THE PARSI
KITCHEN

PRAISE FOR THE PARSI KITCHEN

'Anahita is part of a new generation of Indian chefs who build on the legacies of the past. She is a brilliant chef and will shine even more brightly in the years to come.'
VIR SANGHVI, author of *A Rude Life: The Memoir*

'There is only one thing more beautiful than Anahita Dhondy. Her cooking. Her secret Parsi recipes. And her simple storytelling. Okay, three things.'
FREDDY BIRDY, adman, restaurant designer, artist

'Anahita's passion for the Parsi food of her heritage is at the core of this fascinating book. I'm a little biased as I grew extremely fond of her through her years with us but I'm sure you will really enjoy the stories and the recipes.'
AD SINGH, founder and managing director, Olive Group of Restaurants

'The importance of sustainable food choices is expertly endorsed throughout this engaging read, and Anahita clearly feels a powerful and spiritual connection to food.'
PAUL NEWNHAM, director, SDG2 Advocacy Hub Secretariat

THE PARSI KITCHEN

A Memoir of Food & Family

ANAHITA DHONDY

HarperCollins *Publishers* India

First published in hardback in India by
HarperCollins *Publishers* 2021
A-75, Sector 57, Noida, Uttar Pradesh 201301, India
www.harpercollins.co.in

2 4 6 8 10 9 7 5 3 1

P-ISBN: 9789353578404
E-ISBN: 9789353578411

Printed and bound at
Thomson Press (India) Ltd

f in ⊡ ⚈ HarperCollinsIN

To the strong women in my life

Contents

Introduction

ONE OF MY MOST VIVID MEMORIES is of sitting, cross-legged, on the floor of my mother's kitchen, licking cake batter from a bowl. I was maybe five or six years old, but that was where it all began.

Growing up, I spent almost every free moment in the kitchen, helping out and asking questions. My mother, Nilufer, saw that I had a passion for food and encouraged me to experiment. By the age of eleven, I was icing all the cakes she baked for her home business.

When I turned twelve, I knew that I wanted to be a professional chef and my parents urged me to pursue whatever I was interested in. In class ten, we took a family trip to Aurangabad and along with the Ajanta and Ellora caves, made a sightseeing detour to the Institute of Hotel Management (IHM), where I eventually enrolled.

Ask any eager culinary student and they will tell you that world cuisine is what excites them. Everyone wants to make the most creative sushis and experimental flat breads. Indian food is just shoved to the side. I mean, who's going to study it?

In London, at Le Cordon Bleu (LCB), I had an epiphany. My classmates came from all over of the world, but the one thing they had in common was how proud they were of their ethnicity. It was evident from the respect they showed their traditional food; they revered it. And then there was me: a budding chef who was dismissive of Indian food. I loved to eat it, but I didn't want to cook it.

Until an incident with a pork dish which got me thinking about my own regional cuisine in a way that I never did when I was at home. How strong the flavours are, how complicated the masalas, how ancient the techniques! I asked myself, why am I chasing all these global cuisines when I can do so much with the food back home?

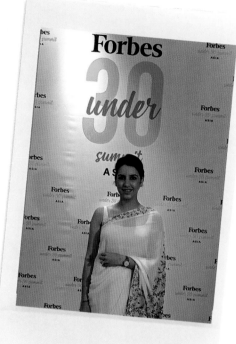

I came back to India, disheartened that I couldn't get a job because of my visa status. My father, Navroze, said, 'When one door closes, another opens.'

And I met ace restauranteur AD Singh. What was meant to be a one-hour conversation stretched to four as we spoke about his to-be-launched project, SodaBottleOpenerWala (SBOW), Parsi food and culture. I was excited because it seemed like a chance to learn more about my roots.

It's been eight years since I made that pivotal decision to take the plunge with Parsi food, and every year I have evolved both as a chef and as a person. I've had the freedom to create, and discover so much about my cuisine, heritage and indigenous ingredients. I've learnt to appreciate Indian food and advocate a place for it among the best in the world. From speaking at a summit to mark United Nations Week in New York to representing India at the Chefs' Manifesto in Stockholm, I've been blessed with so many opportunities.

Making the *Forbes Asia* 30 Under 30 list in 2019 was a huge accomplishment, but what thrilled me even more was that I had the chance to cook for three hundred guests who attended the event.

To think, at age 15, all I wanted was to be a pastry chef!

Who I am is where I come from, so I knew that if I ever wrote a book, I'd want to give readers a peek into everyday life in a Parsi household. A bit of bickering, some amazing anecdotes and, of course, classic recipes handed down through the generations. I hope to take you to a place where you get a glimpse of Parsi culture, my family and my roots, and everything that I've learnt along the way.

Enjoy the journey!

ANAHITA DHONDY

RAVO

*A sweet tale
of sugar in milk*

THERE'S AN AMAZING STORY that every Parsi child has heard from their grandparents or parents, a tale that explains why our community was quick to absorb local practices and traditions on settling in India. An age-old favourite called 'Milk and Sugar', it describes how the Zoroastrians arrived in India and goes a little like this.

When the Parsis first landed in Sanjan, Gujarat, they were met by the local ruler Jadi Rana. Alarmed by the influx of foreigners, Jadi Rana invited my people to make a case for being allowed to enter his province. Legend has it that he used a silver bowl filled to the brim with milk to symbolize how crowded his lands already were, to make it clear that there was no room for newcomers. The Zoroastrian elders added a pinch of sugar to the milk and said, 'The way the milk has not overflowed, but been sweetened, we too will mingle with you and add sweetness to your lives.'

Wisdom won the day, and the Hindu ruler granted permission to the foreigners to settle and practice their faith.

But the license to settle was not unconditional, and the Zoroastrian high priest was asked to explain his faith to the gracious ruler.

The *Kisseh-i-Sanjan* by Dastur Bahman Kaikobad, one of the earliest accounts of the Parsi arrival in India, refers to the conditions Jadi Rana laid down before our ancestors. The foreigners would learn to speak the local tongue (Gujarati). The women would eschew their traditional Persian attire for the Gujarati-style saree drape. The men would give up their arms and swear fealty to the ruler and his successors. There was no talk of conversion, as both Hindus and Zoroastrians believed in the right to practice a faith of one's choice.

Thereafter, the Zoroastrians came to be known as 'Parsis', a term derived from the last port in Persia that they came from—Pars. And honouring this sweet story of assimilation is a classic Parsi milk and sugar dessert called Ravo.

IF YOU FLIP THROUGH a Parsi cookbook, you will see a lot of attention given to fish, chicken, meat, rice, eggs and vegetables. Then there are pickles, chutneys, preserves and relishes. The sweet dish section is smaller, and that is because the Parsi repertoire of desserts is so limited. Most of them are adapted from British dishes like puddings, custards, cakes and cookies. Many are also inspired by traditional Indian sweets; Dar Ni Pori, for instance, is a thicker derivation of a Puran Poli while Badam Pak is similar to Badam Barfi.

Ravo, on the other hand, can be called a purely Parsi dessert because it's inspired by the story of sugar in milk. A little bowl of goodness, it's a dish prepared on auspicious occasions. Ravo made birthdays, anniversaries and festivals more special. Even after Arush and I got married, I've continued the tradition of making Ravo to mark the Parsi New Years. I don't make it on my birthday, though, because Mom still does.

Ravo gets its name from the Gujarati ravo, or suji, and is best described as a semolina and milk pudding. Unlike Kheer, which has a liquid consistency,

A little bowl of goodness, Ravo is a dish prepared on auspicious occasions.

MALIDO, THE PARSI PRASAD

I first heard about Malido, a Ravo-type sweet made with suji, besan and wholewheat, on my trip to the Udvada Atash Behram, the oldest existing fire temple in India. Like an Aate Ka Halwa, Malido is made in ghee, so it's quite heavy compared to Ravo.

The Dasturji's (priest's) wife, Rukshana, told me how they used to make Malido in the olden days. The wheat was coarsely ground, and a sample was sent to the 'ghantiwala' who milled the wheat for the entire village. To create the dough, almost equal amounts of ghee and wheat were kneaded in a thali. The dough is meant to be crumbly, the kind of sandy texture shortbread dough has. It would then be rolled into a big rotla (roti) and roasted on a lakda nu chullu (wood-fired stove) until cooked on both sides and biscuit-coloured. The rotla was then grated—there would be a crunch to it—after which they would add chasni to it and stir till it came together.

That was the traditional Malido recipe technique. Today, just as Ravo is cooked at home, Malido is prepared by the Dasturji's family on auspicious days. It is evenly spread on a thali greased with ghee, sprinkled with dry fruits, and sliced and served with Daran (a small roti) and Papdi (a crispy puri).

On my trip to Udvada in 2016, Rukshana Dastoor showed me how to make Malido.

Malido is prepared in the agiary (fire temple) and served as prasad.

this has the fluffy texture of Halwa. I recall how confused the team at SodaBottleOpenerWala was about the consistency and flavour of the dish when it was first introduced. Accustomed to preparing Halwa with suji and water, it took them time to grasp the idea of a suji and milk dish. You'll rarely find Ravo on a restaurant menu, though. It's usually served at home, during the morning meal, along with an Akuri and other dishes. Picture yourself having dessert with breakfast! In terms of significance, I would place it in the same category as Puran Poli or Khada Prasad. Friends who've eaten Ravo for the first time at my home have always loved it and become diehard fans of it!

LIKE MOST PARSI DISHES, the recipe of Ravo varies from home to home. The original Ravo that I love so much was made by my nani, Vera Ghandhi.

Nani has been a huge inspiration for me, both as chef and entrepreneur. Born and brought up in Ajmer, she moved to Allahabad when she married my

AUNT VILLIE'S MALIDO

Ingredients

65 g whole wheat flour, sifted
25 g maida, sifted
60 g semolina/fine suji, sifted
½ cup milk
250 g sugar
1 cup water
2 eggs, beaten
250 g ghee
½ tsp vanilla essence/nutmeg or cardamom powder/rose water for flavour (optional)
Fried nuts (cashew, almonds, raisins) for garnish

Method

1 Combine the flours in a bowl with milk and ghee. Keep aside for 30 minutes.
2 Cook this mixture over a low flame till it turns light brown. Keep aside.
3 In another pan, heat the sugar and water till the sugar just dissolves (don't make a syrup). Let it cool.
4 Add the cooled syrup to the flour mixture and cook over a low flame till it thickens. Take it off the heat and slowly pour the beaten eggs into the mixture.
5 Put the mixture back on the flame and slowly cook till the preparation is thick.
6 Add the flavours, garnish with nuts and serve.

Ravo may seem like an easy dish to make, but it only gets better with practice. Mom says the secret lies in the love that goes into making it.

grandfather Dossabhoy. She was only sixteen then. A businesswoman with foresight, she was the first person to bring a popcorn maker to Allahabad and had set up a stall at The Palace, their family heritage cinema. After Nana passed away, she took on the management of the cinema hall, the oldest and most prestigious in Allahabad.

Her modern outlook towards the business notwithstanding, Nani was very strict with Mom, Gulzarina Maasi and Darius Mama when they were growing up. Super, super headstrong and extremely disciplined, she is an amazing cook and the best critic. Whenever I ask her to taste something I've made, she doesn't just say 'it's great' or 'nice'. She gives me a proper critique, explaining how I can improve the dish, or what's good and what's not.

Nani, Mom and I follow the same Ravo recipe: one is to one is to four; it's easy to remember in terms of proportion. There are many variations

(Left) Me at my Navjote in 1999; an altar set for Navroz celebrations at home. (Below) Nani and Nana; Nani with Arush and me in 2018.

to it. Growing up, my brother Kurush and I never let Mom add badaam and kishmish (Dad's favourite), so she would often make a half plain, half nutty preparation.

You'll find a lot of Parsis in Mumbai add elaichi and jaifal (nutmeg, a Parsi favourite) to their Ravo. I'm not very fond of it, but I do like to put a little rose water in mine. Mom and Nani use vanilla essence. A cousin maasi of mine adds eggs to make her Ravo nice and fluffy. I also use chironji, an ingredient used in many Parsi desserts. It's very nutty and sweet, and I really like it. I always fry my chironji in ghee and store it. Even in the Lagan Nu Custard, we add chironji on top, before it's baked.

Food preferences change with time and by geography. When I married into a Punjabi household, Kheer made an impact on my Ravo. I now make it with lots of nuts (cashews, almonds, kishmish), which my in-laws love. I don't like it as much, but I make it for them. Just like my immigrant ancestors, I feel blessed to have a new home and am happy to keep my cooking flexible.

Vera's Ravo

preparation time **30 mins** serves **4**

Ingredients

1 cup granulated sugar
4–5 tbsp ghee
1 cup suji
4 cups full-cream milk
1 tbsp rose water (optional)
1 tsp vanilla essence

For garnish
¼ cup each
of chironji seeds,
almond flakes,
cashewnuts, raisins,
tossed in ghee

Method

1 In a pan, add milk and sugar. Warm the milk just till the sugar dissolves.

2 In another pan, heat the ghee and then add the suji. Slowly roast till it becomes a light almond colour.

3 Slowly pour the hot milk over the suji. Keep stirring till it thickens and you can see small bubbles. Make sure the milk is hot or there will be lumps in the Ravo.

4 Add the rose water and vanilla essence.

5 Once the Ravo thickens, pour it into dessert bowls and let it cool. (I usually do one big bowl which gets polished off very quickly!)

6 Garnish with dry fruits. Serve cold or warm, directly from the pan (which is how Arush likes it).

PRO TIPS
Don't brown the semolina; it needs to be a light almond colour, which should take about 10–12 minutes over low heat.

For my friends who insist that there needs to be a crunch in the Ravo (definitely Punjabi blood!), this is the version Arush and his family can't get enough of: Take 300 g cashews, 200 g almonds and 200 g raisins. Cut the cashews and almonds into small slivers, then roast them in a pan with ghee till they are golden brown and crunchy. Make a bed of the browned nuts and raisins on top of your Ravo, completely covering it. Garnish with rose petals.

KAIRI CHICKEN

Mango summers at Dada's house

DINYAR FAREDOON MANCHESHAH PESTONJI Nusserwanji Jivaji Dhondy.
Quite a mouthfull, isn't it? My paternal grandfather cut an imposing figure. As children, his brothers Beji and Kersi gave Dada the nickname 'C.O.'—commanding officer—because he was always ordering them around. Dad and his brother Darius have told us stories about how strict he was.

Growing up, Dinyar's boys were labelled pranksters by people in the locality. Ringing someone's doorbell and then running away before the

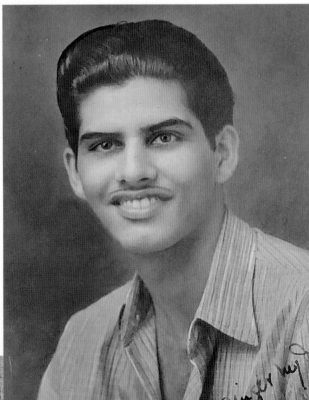

A born commander, Dada was keen to join the navy. He took voluntary retirement when his father's health deteriorated.

unsuspecting person came to the door ... One day, Dinyar was getting a haircut when he overheard someone commenting on his son's mischief. 'How can that mango-eating boy take the mickey out of us?' they grumbled.

Now, you should know that the Dhondy men are all 'aam aadmis'. Chausas, Dussehri or Langda, their love for all types of chusiya mangoes was well-established across town. The comment may have been made in jest, but Dinyar was annoyed to hear his beloved son being ridiculed. He quickly went home, pulled out the largest vessel he could find, half filled it with ice and toppled as many mangoes as he could possibly fit in it. He placed this vessel outside his house for anyone passing by to take a mango from and eat.

The whole town was soon talking about Dinyar's mango philanthropy. A gesture that was both tart and sweet—like the fruit.

MANGOES REMIND ME OF DADA and all the summers Kurush and I spent with him and my grandmother Meher in Allahabad.

It quickly became clear to us kids that Dinyar and Meher Dhondy were the town superstars. Even before Dada met Meher Mumma and went on to have one of the most spectacular love stories I've ever heard, the Dhondy home on Canning Road (now M.G. Marg) was a regular haunt for people from across the city to visit.

'Make room for everyone' seemed to be the Dhondy family motto. Dada had been raised in a rented house in Civil Lines, right behind the famous Hotel Barnett. Modestly spacious, it had housed Dada and his two brothers, Beji and Kersi, their sister, Aban, as well as a distant cousin or two. They were not wealthy, but they were rich in love. Beji, the eldest, was the brightest among the group. Many said his agile mind and caring nature were gifts from god because he had been robbed of the ability to speak or hear. The siblings devised their own 'sign language' to ensure Beji remained abreast of all tales and gossip. Aban was shy and introverted. Kersi was the player and lady slayer on town. If ever there was a smooth operator, it was Kersi.

Dada may have gained a reputation for being a stickler, but Kurush and I only saw his mellow side. He absolutely adored us. When he looked at me and said, 'So, who is my favourite?', I knew he meant me. He told me that

WHEN C.O. SAHIB LOST HIS HEART TO A TEACHER

The story of how Dada and Meher Mumma came together is epic.

Dada's brother Kersi attended an English class in the neighbourhood. It may have been 'baby love' but the googly-eyed boy adored his teacher. Dinyar, only a teenager then, was thunderstruck by the twenty-year-old beauty. He told us, 'She looked like she had stepped out the pages of a classical story, with flowing hair, a perfectly pleated saree and flawless English.' Beji took one look at our C.O. Sahib and signed 'LOVE'.

Kersi gave his brother all the details— she was Meher Patell, daughter of the famous photographer Jamshed M. Patell and regular visitor to the Anjuman—and Dinyar set out to woo his lady love.

Meher was four years older than him and came from an affluent family. But that didn't mean that C.O. Sahib wasn't going to try his best. Over the next four years, he sent flowers and chocolates, made grand gestures that included serenading her from beneath her window ... Until that summer, when she finally smiled at him and their love

story was a go.

However, now that the British were gone, Dinyar wanted to become a C.O. Sahib for real. He decided to join the navy. This news brought the greatest joy to Mr. Patell, who had heard on the grapevine that his angelic daughter was having a fling.

Dinyar and Meher promised to write to each other regularly, but they needed a code to ensure that her parents wouldn't know that they were still in touch.

Cut to five years later on the ship, when Dinyar's senior called him to his cabin and took the mickey out of him. 'I have been informed that you may be a traitor and that you have been selling our information through coded messages to the Italians and the Dutch. Is that true?' he asked.

Dinyar was near tears. 'Sir, this is a sham. Let me face my accuser,' he said.

They threw a file at him and said, 'Explain yourself.'

To his shock and surprise, the file contained his letters to Meher. Dinyar laughed and said, 'Simple rules of English.' He wrote:

H.O.L.L.A.N.D. = Hope Our Love Lives and Never Dies.

I.T.A.L.Y. = I Trust and Love You.

The senior's P.A. whispered, 'Sir, these seem to be love letters.'

Dinyar was given an apology and six months leave to see his lady love. They married, and Dinyar took over his father's small business selling SINGER sewing machines while Meher continued to teach. They set up a happy home, with Beji, and were soon blessed with two sons, Navroze and Darius. Their small family was complete.

when he held me as a baby, I never cried. 'Mota dil wala,' he called me as I was born with my eyes and hands wide open.

Our summers in Allahabad were wonderful, with mangoes being the highpoint of our stay. Ice cream, milkshake, Kairi Chicken … We had a lot of 'mango jam'—literally just mango and sugar—for breakfast. Meher Mumma, a teacher, supervised our holiday homework, but what we really had fun learning was what went on in Dada's tailoring department.

F.M. Dhondy & Sons was a city landmark. It was my great-grandfather's outfit, which Dada took over after voluntary retirement from the navy. During those summer months, we had a routine. In the mornings, we'd clamber on to Dada's bike, feeling all grown-up, and spend our days at the shop. He would read the newspaper while we learnt how to sew. I recall making a little shopping bag for myself! Lunch came from the house in a tiffin carrier, and we all ate together. We went home afterwards and Dada took a nap—precisely 45 minutes—followed by cup after cup of Parsi Choi, and then it was back to the shop.

Dada was an up-to-the-minute kind of guy and had a set time for everything. Much of what we learnt about being disciplined and punctual was from him. He was very patient with us, always explaining things around the shop, answering our incessant questions. We were his shadows—when he had to go somewhere, repair something or buy anything—he always took us along.

(Left) My grandparents with Beji Dada in Allahabad. (Below) Dada and Meher Mumma celebrated their wedding anniversary with us in 2017.

Those long, summer holidays were full of fun, but my favourite memory from back then is of a winter spent in Allahabad. Dada got a special Christmas tree sapling all the way from Bangalore when he visited Mom and Dad, who were posted there. It was a real Christmas tree, not an artificial one, and we enjoyed helping him decorate it. Every year, my grandparents had a big Christmas celebration for the families that lived in their compound and gifts were handed out to all the staff and their children. We'd gather around and sing Jim Reeves songs. It was a simply magical time.

AMBAKALIO

Ingredients

4 medium-sized mangoes
(neither too ripe nor raw)
8–10 baby onions, peeled
2 onions, finely chopped
1 tsp ginger–garlic paste
2–3 green chillies, chopped
2 tsp red chilli powder
1 tsp turmeric powder
50 g jaggery powder
4 tbsp oil
Whole spices (4 cardamoms,
4 cloves, 1-inch cinnamon)
1–2 bay leaves
Salt to taste
Finely chopped coriander for garnish

Method

1 Peel the mangoes. Cut half into thick slices and puree the other half. Set aside.
2 In a pan, heat the oil, add the whole spices, chopped onions and a pinch of salt.
3 Once the onion is golden-brown, add the green chillies and ginger–garlic paste.
4 Add the turmeric and red chilli powder.
5 Add the mango pieces and fry till the raw smells goes away.
6 Add the baby onions, salt and about ¼ cup water, and cook over a low flame till the mango and onions are soft and tender.
7 Add the pureed mango and jaggery powder. Let it simmer till it thickens, then garnish with chopped coriander and cool.

Years later, to honour his memory, we played Jim Reeves on the fourth day of Dada's passing.

THE DHONDY OBSESSION WITH MANGOES lives on in Dad. During the summer months, it is the only fruit you will find in our Gurgaon home. It's Dad who does all the fruit shopping in our family today. He's the one who has taught me how to choose the best of the lot, showing me how to 'touch it like this' and 'smell it like that'. This passion for selecting and sharing fruit is something Dad gets from his father. It's funny how we all seem to carry forward these small, seemingly insignificant behaviours, often without realizing where they stem from. But we are all richer for it.

One his favourite dishes, Ambakalio, dates back to that time of Dada's mango largesse. People had happily helped themselves to the ice-cold fruit on offer outside the Dhondy house in Allahabad, and all the large mangoes were quickly eaten. One day, Darius noticed that the small mangoes at the bottom, though not rotten, were being passed over because of their odd shape. Upset as he was about being left out of his school's sports team, he said, 'They are small, just like me, and will never be picked.'

Dada took one look at him and said, 'Take it to your grandma, and she'll make my favourite dish—Ambakalio.' Reminiscent of instant pickle, it's sweet, sour and a tad spicy.

Ambakalio soon became a Dhondy family favourite, relished on hot days when mangoes were in abundance. 'Zero wastage, boys', Dada said, and many years later, my philosophy remains the same.

Dada passed away a few months before my wedding in 2017. I was devastated, but I consoled myself with the happy memories we had made together. Mangoes remained his favourite, so his request just the day before he passed, left me in tears. He wanted to eat a mango.

Kairi Chicken

preparation time **40 mins** serves **4**

Ingredients

500 g chicken, boneless
3–4 tbsp oil
1 tsp cumin seeds
3 bay leaves
2 medium-size cinnamon sticks
4 medium-sized onions, chopped
4 tomatoes, chopped
2 tbsp tomato puree
(homemade or store-bought)
1 tbsp ginger–garlic paste

2–3 green chillies
Salt to taste
1 tsp red chilli powder
1 tsp coriander powder
½ tsp turmeric powder
½ tsp sambhar masala (p. 193)
1¼ cup chopped ripe mango (reserve the seed)
A pinch of sugar
Chopped coriander for garnish

Method

1 Heat the oil in a pan and add the whole masalas. Let the spices release their aroma.
2 Add the onions and fry till golden brown.
3 Add the ginger–garlic paste and green chilli and fry on medium heat for a few minutes.
4 Add the red chilli, coriander and turmeric powders, and the sambhar masala. Cook the masalas out, then add the tomatoes and tomato puree.
5 Add the chicken and salt and let the chicken cook in an open vessel for about 15 minutes. If it becomes dry, add ½ cup water.
6 Once the chicken is cooked, add the mango (the seed too!) and cook for about 10 minutes.
7 Garnish with coriander and serve hot with pav.

PARSI CHOI & PHETELI COFFEE

Every day
is a fresh start

FROM A SPRINKLE OF SALT to the subtle flavouring of a hot, spiced beverage, it is often the smallest things that make the biggest difference.

My Parsi ancestors, who had settled in Gujarat, may have embraced local ingredients and cooking techniques, but they also sought out familiar flavours. The coastal state, a mineral-rich, water-abundant area, was overflowing with lemongrass and mint, plants with strong aromas, subtle flavours and a freshness that closely resembles those of Persian tea. The flavour immediately clicked and in the hot climate of Gujarat was born a Darjeeling tea spiced with these fragrant herbs. Leeli Chai, as it's known in Gujarati, eventually became a household staple.

Parsi (Leeli) Choi has travelled the world with my people. When I went to London to study at Le Cordon Bleu, I spent days hunting for the perfect tea to satisfy my cravings, but nothing hit the spot. I tried expensive English breakfast teas, blends, Chinese teas ... Then, one day, I was walking past a supermarket and saw a basket of lemongrass and mint on display. My Parsi blood called out to the herbs, so I grabbed a bunch of stalks and leaves along with a packet of Lipton Yellow Label tea. I went home and made myself a pot of Parsi Choi and voila, the hunt was over. I was more than satisfied with my aromatic brew, as it was what I had been longing for. That day, I understood that some flavours are just passed down through your DNA and despite the odds, you will seek until you find them.

I, for one, am obsessed with my morning tea. A perfectly made cuppa gives a fresh start to my day. I think I get it from Dad; he, in turn, gets it from his mother. Meher Mumma was the biggest tea drinker in our family. She would drink some six to eight cups of tea in a day, and her tea times were sacred. In the afternoons, once she was through taking her tuitions, she would lay down on the couch and watch her shows. They were all English shows, I think. At her

4 p.m. tea-time, there would be cookies and cake, and someone would usually drop by to visit. It was almost ceremonial, the high point of her day.

Dad has his own tea tradition. After his 7 a.m. walk, he has a proper English-style tea—with biscuits and the newspaper—in the garden. He doesn't cook; I mean, there are already too many cooks in our house. When Dad enters the kitchen, offering to make something, Mom is like—No, you will just make a mess. I think that's standard for all mothers.

My father isn't a big foodie either, but I would say he is very spontaneous, and experimental when it comes to trying new things. He's the kind of person who doesn't need a main course for dinner or lunch. He's happy with a salad or trying out small portions of different starters. There are times when Mom and I are discussing menus for Anahita and Nilufer's Weekend Kitchen, a delivery service Mom and I started during the COVID-19 lockdown, and he'll come up with an idea which is usually better than the rest.

He always wants chatpata stuff to eat and whips up with his own recipes of masala papad or chakhna. He likes to combine chana dal, kaju, lots of peanuts and spices to have with his drink in the evenings.

PARSI CHOI VERSUS IRANI CHAI

There's a big difference between Irani and Parsi Choi. Today, if you order tea in an Irani café in Mumbai, you'll be served a rich concoction, sticky and sweet. The milk is boiled and boiled, until it becomes as thick as condensed milk. Then they boil the chai (water, sugar and tea leaves) and put just a little bit of this thickened milk on top and serve. Some do say that Irani chai had mawa or khoya in it. The result is creamy yet strong tea. Parsi Choi, on the hand, is lighter and more fragrant with hints of lemongrass and mint.

Irani chai in Mumbai is very different from what is served in Iran. The latter is basically black tea with lots of sugar. We make a version of it at SBOW, it's called Khade Chamach Ki Chai because you can wedge a spoon in the layer of sugar at the bottom of the cup.

I CAN ALWAYS COUNT ON DAD

Mom may be my culinary icon, but Dad has taught me a lot too, the little life lessons you learn over time. I definitely get my discipline, and work ethic, from him. When Kurush and I were growing up, his advertising job meant he had a lot of late nights and work travel. But no matter how late he came in, he'd always be up to take us to the bus stop at 6 a.m.

That time, those few minutes in the morning before the bus came, was ours. He'd correct our pronunciations, help us with our sentences, share some general knowledge titbits and even do a pop quiz with us!

Even after I finished school, I knew I could always count on Dad. I could call him up for anything and, even if he was busy, he would find the time. In college, when I started writing emails, essays and making presentations, I would take him through it first. I'd tell him—This is what I am doing, what do you think, give me your inputs. (Here, too, he lands up editing chapters in my book!) He always helped to make me shine a little better.

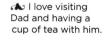 I love visiting Dad and having a cup of tea with him.

The entire tea set-up is very British, you know. We always brew our tea, we don't boil it, and we'll always have batasas, cookies or nankhatai with it. The addition of lemongrass and mint to the tea is how we personalized it.

One Sunday every month, Mom brings out all the different teas we have at home for Dad to create our Dhondy family blend. It's a ritual that dates back a long time, I think. The blend is all his own, and it's very special to me. Even now, after I've married and set up my own home, he sends me a bottle when I run out of it. He insists on making it for me. I think he just feels good that this is something only he can make and that too really well. I mean, I know Mom, or I, can make it too. But it's just this sacred thing that we have. It is very, very special.

Dad's blend is very fragrant; he loves Earl Grey, and I think it lends his tea a lovely floral note. Parsi Choi isn't very strong, but it's usually served with just a few drops of milk. Although, while travelling across Udvada and Navsari, I remember the tea I had was boiled with milk. At home, I usually prepare it with milk on the side, and serve it with sugar or jaggery, which I prefer in the winter.

I married into a Punjabi household, and soon learnt that Punjabis don't take their tea lightly. At breakfast, on my first morning in my new home, I was served tea made from a special family blend that has been passed down through the generations in Arush's family. Now, it would have been rude to say that my tea is better than yours, so I sipped it with a smile. Eventually, I did learn to appreciate it, but my thirst for Parsi Choi persisted.

Then came a day when Arush, who has known me for over fifteen years now, walked in with a handful of lemongrass and mint and a packet of his family tea blend. Together, we were able to concoct the perfect blend of Parsi Choi.

This is the story of how a simple cup of tea has travelled with me around the world. And how, with my migration to a Delhi Punjabi household, yet another influence was absorbed within our Parsi food culture.

But the story is not over. There is coffee too …

THERE ARE TWO KINDS OF PEOPLE in this world—those who love coffee and its simple, elegant flavour, and 'lesser mortals' (Arush's words, not mine!) who have not got the hang of the royal beverage. In all my travels, I have not seen a drink being worshipped more than a cup of coffee. In my food history class at Institute of Hotel Management (IHM), we were taught how this was the drink of kings and that the beans were imported from around the world.

Now, I am not a coffee drinker. It doesn't sit too well with my stomach. But from my days at IHM to my present-day wife status, I am famed for making an extraordinary cup of joe. The trick is one I picked up from Nani. 'Whip it till you can pick it', she used to say. Since whipping or beating the coffee is called 'phetna', in my family we call this Pheteli Coffee. It's more of an Indian, than a Parsi, thing. We like our coffee golden to chocolate brown in colour and with a thick cap of foam on top. This result can be achieved by whisking sugar and coffee, and then adding one spoon of this mixture to hot milk.

What tea was for Meher Mumma, coffee was for Nani. A very sophisticated lady, she always had her elevenses of coffee. While growing up, I found this habit very weird, since she'd already had her breakfast at eight or nine in the morning. Nevertheless, I was always very excited about making her coffee when she came to stay with us. I must have been eleven years old when she taught me how to make it the way she liked. According to Nani, if you could lift your right arm straight up without any pain after beating your coffee, you haven't whipped it enough. Also, if you use a tablespoon instead of a teaspoon, you won't get the same result.

Pheteli Coffee is the only kind of coffee that I can, on occasion, drink. I had a lot of it before my board exams, and Mom still has the only cup I used to make it. In the IHM hostel, I was elected coffee maker when we had to pull late nights. All I needed was instant coffee, sugar, milk powder and hot water from the kettle in our pantry and we'd power through exam prep and project work.

Mom tells me that when she got married, she made Pheteli Coffee for Dad every morning before he left for work. When Arush found out that I am

CHOI PE CHARCHA

Meher Mumma was the one who introduced me to tea. I was staying with her in Allahabad during my summer vacation, and I was very young. She used to drink her last cup of Choi, which was made and kept in a flask, at midnight. After dinner, when everyone else had gone off to bed, she would pour herself a full cup of tea. I'd stay up late with her, and she would pour me a little bit as well. We would sit on the couch together, sipping our Choi and watching TV.

   She is ninety-two today, and she still loves her Choi, though she only has it in the morning now.

48

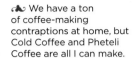

~ We have a ton of coffee-making contraptions at home, but Cold Coffee and Pheteli Coffee are all I can make.

~ Pheteli Coffee is the original Dalgona.

~ The Dasturjis at Udvada love their coffee.

~ My great-grandmother Silla Mumma at tea-time.

a tea drinker, he told me straight up that he is a coffee man, and that he can't leave the house without it. Unfortunately, he also takes an hour to make a cup for himself, so the task has fallen to me. I make Pheteli Coffee perfectly, and he loves my version of it. I always add a drop of vanilla essence, which makes the coffee more aromatic, and lightly sprinkle some cocoa on top. It doesn't really add too much flavour but makes it a little fancier, I would say.

Arush loves his coffee, and has a lot of equipment for it, but he savours what I do with a chamach (spoon). Every time I make it, he says it's better than the last. Funny thing is, I use the exact same recipe. 'Oh, you made it, so it will taste better,' he says. I think he is just being nice. Or lazy!

WHEN I CAME BACK from London and started working at SodaBottleOpenerWala (SBOW), I introduced Parsi Choi on the menu. Boy, did it become a rage. Later, as a tribute to our new discovery, we changed the Choi recipe in the kitchen to the Dhondy-Bhandari family blend.

People were also super excited to order Pheteli Coffee because, you know, there is a kind of nostalgia associated with that one. It gave customers another alternative to the cappuccinos or lattes that are available everywhere now. Pheteli Coffee is what we drank at our parents' or friends' homes. It was the only way of making coffee fancy back then. When Mom saw it on the menu, she was surprised. We toh grew up with this, she said.

Coffee connoisseurs may frown upon the use of instant coffee, but let's be real. We've all been raised on it. So many of us still drink it. And honestly, I feel no drip, pour-over or machine, or even the best quality coffee beans, can compare to this concoction. When you make something from scratch, it's just better.

Dad's Parsi Choi

preparation time **10 mins** serves **4**

Ingredients

3 tsp Dad's special tea blend
1 long stalk of lemongrass,
    crushed or chopped

8-10 mint leaves (or 2 stalks)
1 litre of water
Milk and sugar on the side

Method

1 Boil the water in a kettle or pot.
2 In a teapot, add the tea leaves, lemongrass and mint.
3 Pour the boiling water over the tea mix and close the lid.
   Cover with a tea cosy and let it brew for five to eight minutes
   or until it turns a gorgeous sunny golden colour.
4 Strain into cups and add sugar and a few drops of milk to get
   a creamy colour. Drink hot. Best had with biscuits or Parsi
   bakery cheese batasas!

PRO TIP
To make Dad's special blend, mix 50 g of any Darjeeling leaf tea,
100 g Lipton Yellow Label tea, 20 g Earl Grey tea and 20 g Assam tea in
a clean, dry bowl, and store in an airtight jar or container.

Nani's Pheteli Coffee

preparation time **10 mins** serves **1**

Ingredients

1 tsp instant coffee

2 tsp granulated sugar

1 tsp water

¼ cup boiling water

¾ cup whole milk

A sprinkle of cocoa powder

Method

1 In a cup, combine the coffee powder and sugar.

2 Add 1 tsp water and start whisking (or beating) the mixture with a spoon until it starts looking lighter and foamier.

3 While you beat the coffee, bring the water and milk to a boil separately.

4 When the coffee mixture becomes lighter and foamier, add the water. Continue to beat the coffee to ensure that the water and coffee mixture combine.

5 Now, add the milk. Pour it from a bit of height to create that frothy layer.

6 Lastly, using a teaspoon, give the concoction a little whisk. By now, it should be a frothy almost latte-type mix.

7 Sprinkle some cocoa on top and serve hot.

PRO TIP

This is probably the easiest recipe in the book but don't underestimate it as it does involve some amount of technique. For starters, use only granulated sugar as it whips the best, and ensure that the water used for beating the coffee is precise if you want to get the right texture. Beat the coffee till your right hand tires, and then beat with the left. Keep doing it until the mixture turns a light shade of brown.

AKURI

A Parsi kitchen may
have nothing to eat but it
will always have eggs

Fried, scrambled, beaten, baked ... Parsis eat all preparations of eggs. Dada had a small poultry pen where he kept a couple of hens. He used to eat a raw egg every morning. I remember this incident from when I was around eight and Kurush was three, and we were visiting Allahabad. We were sitting on the steps outside Dada's house, waiting, since we were to go with him to the shop. He came out, holding three or four eggs that he had collected, and placed them in our hands. My brother and I were like, Oh-my-god! We had never held freshly laid eggs; they were really, really warm. Amidst our excited chatter, Dada took one egg, rapped it against the ground and tossed it into his mouth. Kurush and I ran, screaming, like we'd seen a monster. Later, Dada explained how eggs are a great source of strength, and that a freshly laid egg was the best kind to be eaten raw. I was just so shocked.

A Parsi kitchen may be empty but it will always have eggs. They are the backbone of Parsi cooking. Eggs are so multifaceted that, for us, they qualify

BREAKFAST AT UDVADA

During my travels across Gujarat in 2016, I stayed at the Globe Hotel at Udvada. They had a huge breakfast spread, including Akuri, Ravo and an Aleti Paleti, which is basically liver and kidneys tossed in masalas. They have a solid breakfast in these parts, and offal is frequently on the menu. Khurchan, a Parsi-style chicken liver curry, is also popular morning fare.

Parsis are smitten by the idea of a 'high society' breakfast.

as vegetarian. There's a story behind this egg-cellent relationship, one that dates back to our history as immigrants.

Cut to 1666 AD: Surat, India. The British have docked at the silk-laden ports of Gujarat and made friends with the Mughals. Over time, they arrive at a fair understanding of the demographic, terrain, culture and rulers of India. But what they cannot figure out are the Parsis.

At this time, Parsis were the only sect of the Hindustani population that did not follow a caste-based hierarchy and did not fall in the Hindu, Sikh or Muslim segment of the population. We were the only community that possessed no surnames.

From the British point of view, as Hindustanis, we were distinct. From the Parsi perspective, this was the first time we were categorized as Hindustani. From foreigners to locals; this was a giant leap for the community.

We were also traders by the time the British invaded India, and the British were impressed by our entrepreneurial acumen. A budding business relationship often brought Parsi gentlemen to the homes of British officers. (We're talking 1600s—obviously, women were left at home to tend to the chulha instead of socializing. But that is how it was, and even the progressive were not that progressive.) During these early morning visits, Parsi gentlemen were introduced to the famous English breakfast. On a table laden with silverware and crisp cotton napkins, they would find the traditional repast of

My Akuri is pretty good but Mom's is possibly better. Sadly, but truly, that is.

In 2017, at the World on a Plate food carnival in Bengaluru, I made Akuri for the then MasterChef Australia judges George Calombaris, Gary Mehigan and Matt Preston. Same flavours, but I did a modern take. Instead of egg, I used paneer since I find the texture better. I served it with sambhar masala three ways—piped, pureed and brushed—and a garnish of coriander microgreens, alongside thinly sliced pav roasted with a little oil and butter. They loved it!

In 2019, I ordered Akuri while on vacation at Ananda in the Himalayas. I sneaked into the kitchen to show them how to make it properly!

I love Par Eedu, but Paneer Akuri (below right) is a great vegetarian option.

fruit, soft scrambled eggs, beans, jam, marmalade, salted butter and toast. My Parsi ancestors were smitten by this 'high society' breakfast and were quick to introduce it in their homes.

My grandmother told me that the British always had a very lavish morning spread because, as the saying goes, you should breakfast like a king. It's a practice that we Parsis borrowed from the British. In my parents' home, breakfast has always been quite a big deal. As kids, we never had to ask for it. Sleepy-eyed, we made our way to the table and Mom would put fried eggs on our plates; sometimes there would be rotli, other times there was bread or toast. If Mom was in a mood to make something fancier, then it would be Akuri for breakfast. It's the same for most Parsi homes, I imagine.

A creamy scrambled egg, Akuri is and always has been the ace in a Parsi cook's repertoire. Every family has its own preference for how runny they like their Akuri. I enjoy a soft scramble, more on the cooked side, but Mom prefers it even softer. The actual technique for preparing Akuri is to fry the masala and then turn the gas off before adding the egg. The pan has enough heat for the egg to cook, and that's how Mom makes it. I, on the other hand, add the egg and cook it a little before turning the gas off. I always add half a teaspoon of butter into the Akuri mixture and top it with chopped dhaniya. That's how I like it; Nani, on the other hand, has a totally different way of doing it from Mom and me. Her Akuri is a little more solid, like a Bhurji.

It's such a homely recipe that no one will invite you over specially to have Akuri. It's not something that I would make if I was entertaining people at home. Likely, you'll be served Akuri in someone's house only if you are staying with them, and then too it's made as a breakfast treat especially for you, to your specification, eggs to order. To think, I've only eaten Akuri at Gulzarina Maasi's, Nani's and Meher Mumma's homes.

Our Akuri at home was a favourite with many people, especially Dad's friend Uncle Brajesh (Betu). Before setting out from his New Jersey home and arriving in India, his instructions were clear—he wanted Akuri on Toast. Mom would have his favourite food ready and many a times I chipped in when she was away visiting Nani.

Akuri also has variations. There's the regular Akuri, which is my favourite. Then there is the Leela Lasan Nu Edu, a seasonal preparation made with green garlic, spring onion, green chilli and chopped dhaniya. I'd compare it to truffle scrambled eggs, but with heightened flavours. It's white—a light green, almost—soft, fluffy, and just delicious.

The third type is the Bharuchi Akuri, served at weddings and all the Bhonus (feasts), etc. It's the fanciest and heaviest recipe, loaded with dry fruits and nuts (almonds, cashews and the Parsi favourite—raisins!). Some people put mawa as well. I hate it, but most Parsis love it.

The fourth is a version we've invented for vegetarians—the Paneer Akuri, which is basically grated paneer with Akuri masala.

EVERYONE HAS A SPECIFIC way they like their eggs. Kurush, for instance, refuses to eat Akuri. He likes his eggs very plain, with no masala. I don't think he even salts them. At breakfast, it was always Akuri for everyone and fried eggs for my brother.

But then, nothing compares to a good fried egg in ghee. It's a Parsi favourite. There was a time when everyone—my grandparents, uncles, aunts—would cook with ghee; it was a fat that they used in all their cooking. Then refined oil took over and all the advertisements said it's amazing, great, flavourless, light, etc. Ghee was put into the bad fat category until, suddenly, it made a comeback. Today, we know that flavoured oils (mustard, sesame, peanut) from different parts of India are actually good for you. Now everyone's back to having eggs in ghee. It has the best kind of flavour and fat, in my opinion.

Eggs are an absolute all-rounder on the Parsi menu. We use eggs in EVERYTHING. I mean, you won't find a dessert which is eggless because we love eggs so much. Lagan Nu Custard, Caramel Custard, Mawa Cake ... Eggs also feature at lunch if you are doing any cutlets, patties or fried stuff. At tea-time, egg sandwiches are very popular. At dinner, a lot of leftovers are reused, and eggs add protein to the meal.

Repurposing leftover food is part of our food culture, and that's why the Par Eedu is so famous. Roughly translating to 'egg on top of everything', this is a quintessential Parsi dish where anything in the fridge is used to create a new dish. Any sabzi, or even wafers which have become soggy, can be topped

QUICK-FIX AKURI MASALA

It's the texture, and the masala combination, that differentiates Akuri from Anda Bhurji. Akuri masala is a type of pyaaz-tamatar bhuna paste seasoned with red chilli, haldi and sambhar masala. Some people add jeera, dhaniya and garam masala powders as well.

You'll always find two or three types of pastes in a Parsi kitchen for jhatpat cooking. In the mad morning rush, you can just take out the paste, put two spoons of it in a pan and scramble it with eggs. Or you can spread it over toast and eat as you dash out of the house.

The Akuri masala is both long-lasting and versatile. It can be used for any sabzi—alu gobi, kaddu—and finished with a tadka. I often use it for Prawn Patio. It saves you the trouble of having to bhuno masala every time you cook.

with an egg and eaten. Take a dry bhindi ki sabzi, for instance. I'd add a little water to a pan and wait for it to start bubbling. Then, I'd add the bhindi, make a little well and crack the eggs into it. What happens is the yolk kind of sits there and the white spreads out. For a small pan, I'd use two eggs; three if it's a bigger pan and then cover it with a lid. To prevent burning, the older generation of cooks would cover the egg with a plate topped with water before putting a lid over the pan. A baked egg, like a Shakshuka.

Every Parsi has a Par Eedu favourite; I have three. Non-vegetarian would be Kheema Par Eedu; Tamota Par Eedu, which is a simple base of spiced tomatoes topped with egg, and Bheeda Par Eedu (a bhindi sabzi leftover) are my vegetarian picks. People rarely think of bhindi and egg as a combination, but it's delicious. In Hong Kong, I remember having this amazing truffle egg

Nothing teaches patience like cooking, especially when it's your first time. Not knowing what your final product is going to look like and still going at it requires another level of self-restraint that not every activity can teach you. Apply that to your life or your cooking, just remember you heard it here first.

scrambled with very thin slices of bhindi in it. It really hit the right spot.

Omelette, or Poro, also plays a big part in Parsi cooking. Dad is an omelette lover, and Mom makes a really good spicy Poro. In summers, she always puts kachcha aam in all her omelettes. Raw mango chopped with the usual masala (especially Mom's sambhar masala) and the other omelette ingredients—pyaaz, tamatar, dhaniya and mirchi—tastes amazing. It's also a very Parsi thing to do, adding a sweet or sour element to any dish.

Mom's always done a lot of omelette variations, depending on the ingredients that we have at home. We do a lot of eggs with cheese and truffle oil, spiced with a little green chilli. Mushroom and cheese is another great combination to be had with bacon and sausages. I'd also recommend caramelized onions and cheese—I keep a jar of onions in my fridge. If I have leftover grilled chicken or chicken loaf, I like to shred it and toss it in.

EGGS ARE SO INTEGRAL to Parsi cooking that I thought carefully about how to introduce them at SodaBottleOpenerWala. We wanted to do a menu which was a mix of home-cooked Parsi favourites and something that you get in an Irani café and some clubs as well. Akuri was definitely our first option; we've done several varieties of Par Eedu over the years. We started off with Bheeda Par Eedu, then we did a kheema followed by a sausage one; for a Kheema Khari Par Eedu, we add crumbled khari biscuits. For the vegetarians, there was a Mushroom and Cheese Par Eedu with spinach.

For breakfast, we came up with different Poros with fun names. For instance, there's an Angry Poro—one that has a lot of chilli— and a Meat Lover's with bacon, ham and sausages in it. There's also the Wrestler Omelette, which has got eight eggs in it because it's named after an Iranian wrestler who ate that many.

The other day, we were debating whether we should do a DIY brunch box for the Weekend Kitchen. We give you ends—Akuri masala, homemade bread—and you make your own eggs. Then Arush pointed out that people wouldn't know the correct texture of Akuri, and that they'd wind up making Bhurji instead. There's this whole debate about how the texture of Akuri must be really soft and spreadable. A lot of people love it and are very anal about it (Arush, you think?) while others hate it because it is so soft. They prefer it less kachcha. I don't see what the fuss is about, really. After all, they're the ones who are going to eat the eggs. They can make their own rules!

LEELA LASAN NU EEDU
Green Garlic Scrambled Egg

Ingredients

4 eggs
1½ tbsp young green garlic, finely chopped
1 tsp garlic, finely chopped
1 tbsp spring onion, finely chopped
½ tsp fresh coriander, finely chopped
1-2 green chillies, fine chopped
½ tsp oil
2 tbsp butter
Salt and pepper to taste

Method

1 Melt the butter in a pan, and gently sauté the garlic and green chillies.

2 In a bowl, beat the eggs till they are frothy. Add salt and pepper.

3 Pour the eggs into the pan and mix with the garlic and chillies till the egg is softly set. Switch off the gas and add the spring onion and coriander. Serve on hot buttered toast.

Add a lot of butter to your hot Akuri—it tastes amazing and gives the dish that velvety look.

Akuri

preparation time **20 mins** serves **2**

Ingredients

3 eggs (4 would be greedy)
2 tbsp oil
2 medium-sized onions, finely chopped
2 medium-sized tomatoes, finely chopped
½ tsp ginger–garlic paste (you can use chopped ginger–garlic as well)
1 green chilli, slit and finely chopped (take 2 if you like it spicy like I do)

1 tsp sambhar masala (p. 193)
½ tsp turmeric powder
½ tsp red chilli powder
Salt and pepper to taste
1 tbsp butter
Fresh coriander for garnish
2 slices of toasted bread, slathered with butter

Method

1 Heat the oil in a non-stick pan on high. Add the onions and chillies, and fry till brown. Add the ginger–garlic paste and cook for a few more minutes.

2 Add the sambhar masala, turmeric and red chilli powder. After tossing everything around in the pan for a couple of minutes you will have a rich, dark masala. If you think it looks dry, don't worry—just add some water to it.

3 Now, add the tomatoes to the pan and stir until they cook and thicken. (This would take about 5–8 minutes.) Your paste is ready—you can either cool and store it or make your eggs.

4 Break the eggs in a bowl, add salt and pepper and whip them.

5 This is the crucial step—turn the burner down to the lowest heat or, as we call it, sim. Gently pour the whipped eggs into the pan, running your spatula through the eggs. Keep stirring until it becomes the colour of the sun at dusk.

6 After three or four minutes of stirring, increase the heat. The egg will start to cook quicker, so you need to stir faster. This is when I add coriander to my eggs.

7 In another two to three minutes, your egg will be ready— runnier than Bhurji or a scrambled egg. Toast some bread, spread with butter and Akuri, and enjoy.

PORK VINDALOO

A spicy cure for homesickness

DURING THE COURSE OF MY TRAVELS, I have had several epiphanies. One of them was that the logical thinking of the West may be slightly off when it comes to the spices we use in our daily cooking.

When I was studying at Le Cordon Bleu (LCB) in London, I was led to believe that spices are used to cover up the faults in basic ingredients. So, if you cook with fresh and well-cut ingredients, salt and pepper are all the flavouring that you need. I embraced this principle as my truth. After all, it was reiterated by the master chefs of the college, whose technique and style just blew me away.

The atmosphere at LCB is not what one might imagine—it's the IIT of the food world, so every day is hard. A test, a battle. I am proud to say that each one of my classmates emerged victorious, all thanks to the training we received there.

The master chefs at LCB taught us—students of the Grand Diplôme course—a new technique every day, from how to hold a knife to cutting out a perfect filet mignon. Eighty per cent of the classes were practical and, after a one-hour class with the chef, we would be given an ingredient list and asked to make the dish. At times, we'd prepare up to three recipes a day.

We spent long hours in the hot and cold kitchens, and often had classmates fainting, sometimes even breaking down, under the pressure. In class by 7 a.m., theory till 1.30 p.m. followed by practicals till 4.30 p.m. Back at home, I had to prep ingredients for the next day, washing my chef's coat, ironing my chef whites, cleaning and sharpening my knives, trial runs for those looming taste tests ... and the day was done. I barely managed to call the people I loved back in India and when I did catch them, I was greeted with yawns (time difference!) and the usual 'you are too busy for me' complaints. I had become the evil other in a long-distance relationship with my mother and boyfriend.

My flatmate, Nitya, was studying at the London School of Fashion. We were both students on a budget, and ate leftovers from what I cooked at school for dinner.

The goal of Le Cordon Bleu is to produce informed, adaptable and efficient chefs who will be able to find their feet in an ever-changing industry. In short, it is a school of culinary warriors.

I always wanted to study abroad to gain perspective on the international food scene. My LCB graduation ceremony in 2013 was such a memorable day.

This cycle was driving me crazy and the London weather wasn't helping. Eventually, I broke down.

I may have been living my dream in one of the greatest cities in the world, surrounded by some of the best culinary minds ... Yet I was yearning for my people, my home. I was 'sad Dhondy', worried that I wouldn't be able to handle the pressure.

On one such dark day, our master chef tasked us with preparing Pork Fillet with Prunes, Stuffed Paris Mushrooms and Potatoes Dauphine. When assigned a dish as part of our practical class, we were asked to cook a portion for two, just in case we couldn't properly plate on the first try. While the first, or presentation, portion was plated and subjected to a taste test, we were allowed to take the second, or 'safety', portion home. Now, understand that this was a fine French dish where the meat was the hero; the prunes and potatoes were just accents. I diligently followed the recipe step-by-step. My pork was cooked beautifully, and my sauce was salted and peppered just enough to ensure it was not too sweet. It was the perfect texture and balance, and both my plates—presentation and safety—looked identical.

As I cooked it, though, I felt as if it was missing something. To my surprise, when it was served, the chef loved it. He invited the other staff members and students to taste it. I was elated by all their praise.

However, that niggling sense of dissatisfaction remained. Do you ever get that feeling in the pit of your stomach, when you are rewarded for your work, but you know it is not perfect? That's how I felt—like a hack, grabbing praise for something that I was not completely happy with. The flow of tears started as soon as I left the building.

The walk back home that day is one I will never forget, because it made me the chef I am today.

❧ E.F. Kolah & Sons and E.H. Kolah & Sons are two famous families in Navsari who have been making Kolah vinegar since 1885.

In London, I realized that I could make the most beautiful lamb or pork chops and any kind of potatoes, displaying a lot of technique. But ultimately, flavour is king. It's that taste in your mouth that will keep you coming back for more.

I fell and bruised my knee. I cried from the pain of my fall. I missed Mom. Arush's calming voice. Dad's resolute advice. I had had enough of the new. I wanted something I knew.

My flatmate, Nitya, who was at home, realized something was very wrong when I walked in bruised and wailing. I got a hug, a pep talk and a vodka shot, and she refused to eat until I ate. After twenty minutes of consoling me, she asked for the pork I had brought home.

As I watched Nitya poke through that plastic takeaway box of pork, I just knew I could not let someone I loved eat a dish that I had cooked and didn't feel one hundred per cent sure about.

I'll never forget her aghast expression as I took the box from her, walked into the kitchen and washed the sauce off the pork. Then, I took out the masala kit Mom had packed for me when I left India, and attempted a recipe I had never cooked before, but one that resonated with my personality, heritage and character.

Mom's Pork Vindaloo.

VINDALOO IS A DISH PREPARED in a lot of Parsi homes, a legacy handed down from generations of Goan cooks.

Parsi Vindaloo is the same as the Goan version on many counts—we use red chillies, garlic, ginger, whole spices (cloves, cardamom, cinnamon, turmeric) too—except one. While Goans use coconut or toddy vinegar, a typical Parsi Vindaloo is made with Kolah vinegar. The base of this vinegar is sugarcane—it tastes like tart molasses and has a colour that is as stark. What balsamic vinegar is to Italian food, sugarcane vinegar is to Parsi food!

MASALA MANTRA

Vindaloo has a distinct taste. The spices—Kashmiri red chilli, cumin seeds, coriander seeds, black pepper, cloves, cinnamon and green cardamom—give the dish its fiery kick and colour. The sourness of the vinegar and tamarind balance out the hot flavours. There's a technique you need to follow while roasting the spices: be sure to roast them according to size. Use oil instead of dry roasting them. The oil lubricates the masala and you don't need water to grind, which means you can keep the masala for up to a year. Remember, never store the masala in a plastic container or cling wrap. The acidity in the vinegar will cut right through it. Stick to airtight glass containers.

I should add I'm not a stickler for using Kolah vinegar in my recipe. It's the khada (whole) masalas that are key to this dish. The best meat for Vindaloo would be good quality, fatty pork. It needs to be cooked really well and slowly; in India, the best way to do that is to pressure cook it.

At home, Mom always makes Pork Vindaloo on a Sunday, and serves it with bread. That evening, after class in London, that Vindaloo was the taste of home I craved. So I called Mom for the recipe. Later when I called to tell her that it had come out really well, guess what she said? 'Yes, obviously. I gave you the recipe. What did you expect? Enjoy it.'

MOM!

She visited me in London soon after and made Vindaloo for my friends. It was much tastier than mine, and they loved it so much that we made plans to set up a stall in Borough Market to sell Vindaloo and pav.

That never happened, but over the years (and with the help of Chef Aneesh at SBOW, Hyderabad), I think my Vindaloo paste has become better than hers.

AS NITYA AND I SAT DOWN with our bowls of Pork Vindaloo and bread, I was still crying a little bit. What I know now that I didn't then was that this dish was going to be life-changing for me.

In London, I realized that I could make the most beautiful lamb or pork chops, or gravy and mash, or any kind of potatoes displaying a lot of technique. But ultimately, flavour is king. It's that taste in your mouth that will keep you coming back for more. I think that's why that Vindaloo dinner was a turning point for me.

I began finding the food I was making at school too bland for my palate. So, I started making a chatpatta, more Indianized version of the food I would bring back home.

It all began with that Pork Vindaloo, that had made it clear an emotional connection to food was important for me. That's how I found my culinary niche as a regional cuisine chef.

I didn't know that this dish was going to be life-changing for me.

Pork Vindaloo

preparation time **1 hour** serves **4–6**

Ingredients

For the Vindaloo paste

200 g Kashmiri red chillies

2–3 bulbs of garlic, peeled and chopped

1 big piece of ginger, peeled and chopped

2 tbsp cumin seeds

2 tbsp coriander seeds

1 tbsp black peppercorn

1 tsp cloves

2–3 medium-size cinnamon sticks

2 tsp turmeric powder

Salt to taste

350 ml Goan (or any other type) vinegar

3 tbsp jaggery

1 tsp green cardamom

1 tbsp tamarind paste

½ cup oil

1 tsp green cardamom

Note This recipe makes 1 kg Vindaloo masala

For the pork

1 kg pork belly/shoulder,
cut into curry pieces

200 g Vindaloo paste
(depending on how spicy you want it)

¼ cup oil

4 large onions, sliced

1 tsp ginger–garlic paste (optional)

A handful of fried onions (optional)

Method

To make the masala

1 Soak the red chillies in a pot of hot water for 3–4 hours. This softens the chillies and makes it easier to grind them.

2 Heat the oil in a pan and roast the masalas till they are fragrant. I like to roast the smaller masalas (cumin, coriander, peppercorns, cloves, green cardamoms) together but Mom prefers dry roasting them separately. Leave them to cool on a plate.

3 Lightly fry the garlic, ginger and turmeric, as that improves the shelf life of the masala.

4 Combine the roasted masalas, chillies, garlic, ginger, vinegar, jaggery, tamarind and salt in a mixer and grind till a smooth paste. Store in a glass jar or bowl and refrigerate.

To make the pork

1 Marinate the pork with Vindaloo masala a day ahead for best flavour.
2 In a pressure cooker over medium heat, add the oil and the sliced onions and bhuno till brown.
3 Add the ginger–garlic paste, and the marinated pork and sauté till the pieces are nicely seared and brown. (If you're not using the paste, then just sear the pork.)
4 Add water (about 1 cup) and close the cooker lid. Cook for 6–8 whistles, till the pork is tender.
5 Garnish with fried onions and serve hot with fresh onion rings, chopped coriander, lemon and freshly baked pav.

PRO TIPS

If you're cooking with pork, it's best to marinate it for at least twenty-four hours.

You can swap the pork with jackfruit or paneer to make a vegetarian version. Cooking times will differ.

This is a versatile masala, and can be used like chilli garlic sauce, for instance. I've made Chicken Burritos and a Pumpkin and Okra Coconut Milk Curry with it.

PATRA NI MACHCHI

Health and a
wealth of flavours

'KHAVANU, PIVANU, MAJJA NI LIFE'—eat, drink and enjoy your life—
is the Parsi motto. We associate our food with celebration and love and that
shows in it.

Largely unaffected by the healthy food trend that has changed the way
people are eating the world over, we are still gorging on our cheese batasas,
Dal Ma Gosht and Tareli Machchi. Everyone's just eating and chilling, fondly
watched over by their Parsi mummas.

Well, not everyone.

Take the case of the Mastiwala family, whom
I know and love. As their name suggests, Beji
Uncle, Bapsi Aunty and their two sons, Noshir and
Hormuz, are a fun-loving bunch. They also loved
to indulge themselves, to put it mildly. They would
eat and drink without restraint. And when I say drink,
I mean a 'bawa' peg—one or two for starters, one with
the meal and a couple before the end of the night. A peg is
30 ml, a large or double is 60 ml, a Patiala is 90-120 ml (five
fingers). A bawa peg—that's five fingers spread in the glass ... any
glass. Clearly, the name of the game was 'last man standing' and it
was usually Beji Uncle who won.

For Bapsi Aunty and Almeida, the Mastiwala's household help,
the things Beji Uncle and the boys ate with their drinks was a bigger
concern. A couple of plates of Chicken Farcha and their favourite
Banana Leaf, Coconut and Coriander Chutney as starters, two plates
of rice with Dhan Dar Patio or Dhansak each for dinner, and a bowl of
Lagan Nu Custard or Ravo for dessert was ordinary fare. On this diet, it's
no wonder that the Mastiwala men had each gained fifteen kilos within a
span of months.

The family was pretty okay with this—they were rich merchants, after all, and to the victor go the spoils. But a visit to the Surat Club, where other members started calling them Bejan 'Gubarawala' (balloon) and sons, put a damper on their enthusiasm!

Now, drinking, Bapsi Aunty could tolerate. Disrespect, she could not.

Troubled by the family's immense weight gain, Bapsi Aunty turned to Almeida for help. Almeida, a Goan lady with more character than a George R.R. Martin novel, ran a tight ship and, as expected, had a solution to the problem. She suggested a change in diet that Beji Uncle and the boys wouldn't notice.

On day one, they presented the men with fresh tomatoes in olive oil to munch on with drinks. At the sight of the tomatoes, Beji Uncle started wailing. Have I lost all my riches that my wife can't afford to feed me a cooked snack with a measly drink?

The next day, Bapsi Aunty served cottage cheese sautéed with some fresh-cut tomatoes. Hormuz made wild allegations against the staff. Who has eaten all the meat in the house that us wage-earning men are left with vegetarian food, he railed.

Day three, Almeida steamed some basa fish as a starter with drinks. Not much to complain about, but Noshir did say the 'dry fish' left him bereft of all hope.

The two women were canny enough to recognize that, for their weight management plans to succeed, they would have to find a dish that knocked the men's socks off. That razzle-dazzle creation was steamed chamna (Gujarati for silver pomfret) with their favourite green chutney. The fish preparation of Parsi dreams, best known as Patra Ni Machchi.

Fortunately, the Mastiwala men couldn't find much to crib about in the fish and quit grumbling about the subsequent alterations made to their daily

diet. And thus, Bapsi Aunty and Almeida—with a little help from their friend Patra Ni Machchi—were quietly successful in bringing their men down to size. For the world at large, however, the disappearance of the potbellies came to be known as the 'Mastiwala Mystery'.

I love Patra Ni Machchi, not only because it solved the Mastiwala Mystery in my mind, but also because it is one of the most delectable Parsi dishes, one that epitomizes how adaptable and malleable our cuisine is. Created from locally sourced ingredients, it is an epic masterpiece that is present on Parsi menus everywhere today, no matter the occasion.

This is a dish that is the perfect tribute to the coastal area where we put down roots, the best blend of the ingredients that are available in abundance across Maharashtra and Gujarat. You've got coconut, coriander, mint, banana leaves and fish. It's always made with pomfret, because it absorbs the chutney beautifully. You can either use chamna or a black pomfret steak. Personally, I prefer the smaller, silver pomfret. It's always best to use fish with the bone in because it adds flavour and ensures the flesh retains its moistness. Of course, I've used boneless fish and it still comes out perfect.

The green chutney is a staple in every Parsi household and used in a variety of ways. One of my fondest childhood memories is watching the chutney being made on the sil-batta (grinding stone) in Nani's Allahabad house. It was all done on the ground, on wooden patlas (small stool).

There is no flavour that compares to chutney prepared using a sil-batta. Sprinkle a little water as you crush, and you'll get a moist paste. Unlike a mixer-grinder, the sil-batta helps coax out the subtle flavours and fragrances from ingredients.

Mom has one at home in Gurgaon, but nobody uses it. It's too much of an effort—lifting, washing and cleaning it. I draw the line at a mortar and pestle! Stone grinding the chutney isn't the only tradition consigned to the past. I genuinely don't see a lot of people making Patra Ni Machchi at home today. It's an elaborate cook, and a little tedious, if you ask me, which is why you'll see it is usually served during festivals, on special occasions and at fancy dinners. In most homes these days, you'll find Tareli Machchi (fried fish) is the more popular choice. (For recipe, see p. 175)

Patra Ni Machchi wasn't a dish Mom made very often, so around the time I was planning the menu for SodaBottleOpenerWala (SBOW), I sourced the chutney recipe from her catering partner Jaloo Aunty. (Back in early 2010,

GREEN CHUTNEY GOODNESS

Green chutney is an all-time favourite Parsi condiment. Apart from Patra Ni Machchi, in Parsi homes, this chutney is used to make Stuffed Pattice. I love making sandwiches of soft milk bread with the sides cut off, using this chutney, butter and cheese as spreads. It always reminds me of evenings spent at the National Centre for the Performing Arts during my childhood trips to Mumbai. It's also a great accompaniment with Moong Dal Bhajia. So it's a very versatile chutney overall. Made with fresh coconut, coriander leaves, mint, roasted cumin, green chillies, sugar, salt and lemon juice, it will keep for about 3-4 days. You'll always find a bottle in my fridge.

she and Mom ran a catering service for small functions held by Parsi families in Delhi.) I tweaked it to make the chutney slightly sour and spicy, but it is largely her recipe that we use at the restaurant. I also marinate the fish with a little bit of lemon juice, salt and garlic paste to enhance the flavours of the dish.

It's very weird, but I genuinely have not found the perfect pairing for Patra Ni Machchi. A lot of people eat it with rotli (thin chapattis), others prefer it with rice. At SBOW, I lobbied hard to serve Patra Ni Machchi with Coconut Millets, which is more nutritious than rice. Sadly, it didn't take and isn't on the menu anymore, but it was a great pairing. I like to have it with a lemon-coconutty kind of rice on the side. It gives that citrus balance to the dish. Or, something with a very subtle flavour. Never pav!

WHILE OUR IRANIAN ROOTS REMAIN strong, the extent to which Parsi food is influenced by Gujarati and Maharashtrian culinary traditions became

∼ Patrail, spiced rolls of colocasia (arbi) leaves, is another Gujarat-inspired Parsi favourite.

∼ Vegetarians can do a Patra Ni Paneer (below), with a slice of paneer layered and steamed. It comes out really nice.

You can also make Patra ni Machchi with any other fleshy fish, like rawas or singhara. Even a John Dory or sea bass would work. But the one that's perfect is chamna.

apparent to me when I travelled to Gujarat in 2016.

There is a significant difference between the ingredients available to those of us who migrated inland and up north, and those who settled on the coast. Take tender jowar seeds, or ponkh, and lima beans (which are soaked and peeled to make Vaal Ni Dal), for instance. Both ingredients are hard to source in Gurgaon. But we've grown up eating them during our summers in Allahabad and Mumbai, so they are sorely missed.

Seafood, coconut, green beans … these fresh ingredients were embraced by Parsi settlers. Kopra (dried coconut) is used in Parsi Prawn Curry and to make Kopra Pak (a type of coconut barfi) and Kopra Chapat (a Parsi pancake stuffed with coconut).

Banana leaves, which I believe are among the best ingredients you can use for cooking, are also available in abundance. Unfortunately, living up north, it's so hard to source them! At the restaurant in Delhi, we pay ₹ 25 per leaf, whereas at the Mumbai outlet, we get them for free. One of the first things I did when I moved into my own house in Gurgaon was plant my own banana tree. Now, whenever I make Patra Ni Machchi, I don't have to ask permission to cut leaves from someone else's tree!

Coastal ingredients that have found their way on to the Parsi menu have an additional benefit—they are light and nutritious and balance out our meat-and-spice heavy cuisine. Patra Ni Machchi, for instance, is a very lightly flavoured preparation, an anomaly in a culinary tradition that isn't otherwise associated with healthy cooking.

As a chef, I am trying to change that by pairing Parsi flavours with healthier ingredients like millets and other plant-based foods that I champion. People do cuss me out for this initiative, saying, 'Oh, you are promoting bird feed,' but even the Mastiwala men can't deny the benefits of a cleaner diet. And if there was ever a time to acknowledge the importance of working towards a healthy and sustainable food future, it is now.

Patra Ni Machchi

preparation time **1 hour** serves **4**

Ingredients

For the fish

500 g fish (boneless,
cut into 10–12 pieces)
Juice of 2–3 lemons
Salt to taste
1 tsp red chilli powder
1 tsp turmeric powder
4 banana leaves

For the chutney

1 cup fresh coconut, finely grated

2 cups fresh coriander (with stem)
$1/4$ cup mint leaves
2 tbsp sugar
6–8 large cloves of garlic, peeled
5–6 green chillies
1 tsp cumin seeds
Salt to taste
Ice water to blend

For the garnish

Lemon slices

Method

1 Marinate the fish pieces with salt, lemon juice and spice powders. Keep aside for 1–2 hours.
2 Blend all the ingredients for the chutney in a mixer. Keep aside.
3 Soften the banana leaves by passing them lightly over a low flame. Then, cut away the stalk. Cut the leaf into squares large enough to wrap the fish pieces.
4 Arrange the leaf on a clean surface. Apply one layer of chutney, then place the fish on it. Cover the fish with another layer of chutney.
5 Fold the sides of the leaf over the fish and secure the parcel with the help of a toothpick or string.
6 Steam the parcel in a rice cooker or idli steamer for 10 minutes or until the fish is cooked. Garnish with lemons and serve with onion rings.

PRO TIP
Never add water to chutney, only a couple of cubes of ice. That helps the chutney, or for that matter any puree (pesto, for example) retain a vibrant green colour.

IF YOU'RE MAKING PATRA NI MACHCHI FOR THE FIRST TIME

There are two very important things to keep in mind. One is getting the consistency of the chutney right. Don't make it too watery—it needs to be nice and pulpy so that it can be spread in a thick layer, and be evenly absorbed by the fish while it is being steamed.

The second thing is the cooking technique. While you can steam the fish, double-boiler style, there is another method that involves tying the fish parcel and dunking it in water. If you do that, make sure you've wrapped the fish perfectly tight or the chutney will ooze out. Personally, I prefer steaming it because it's a more controlled set-up and the fish cooks better.

What I do, if I'm using an entire small silver pomfret, is steam it on one side first for four minutes and then flip the parcel and steam it for another four minutes. Then, I use a toothpick to check if it needs a couple more minutes. Usually, a small silver pomfret will cook in 10–12 minutes.

DHAN DAR PATIO

A little dal goes a long way

CHEF THOMAS KELLER OF The French Laundry once said, 'A recipe has no soul. You, as the cook, must bring soul to the recipe.'

Anyone who has had the privilege of sampling Dolly Lakrawala's cooking will agree with Keller. More than skill or temperament, it is the love in her heart that transforms a simple repast into a magnificent meal.

Tucked away in a quiet corner of South Mumbai, the opulence of Dolly's home took me by surprise. It was the first house in Mumbai I had been to that had a driveway and garden! I rang the doorbell, half expecting Mrs Raichand of *Kabhi Khushi Kabhie Gham* fame to appear, thali in hand. Instead, I was greeted by Gordon, Dolly's crusty old Goan caretaker.

Over tea and cheese batasas, Dolly, an effervescent forty-year-old, shared the story of her most cherished Parsi dish—Dhan Dar Patio. She said, 'As our forefathers made the long journey from Iran to Surat, they didn't have much to subsist on. The lentils were mostly just water, so the priests started mashing it together to make a kind of ground lentil soup to go around.'

Comforting, simple and so easy to digest, Dhan Dar is to Parsis what Dal-Chawal is to non-Parsis. As Dada would say, 'In the old days of the British Raj, we used to eat daul (sic), rice and curry for breakfast, lunch and dinner.' In Gujarati, Dhan stands for rice, Dar for dal. Patio, the third in this trilogy of flavours, is taken on the side like an achaar. A sweet, sour and spicy dish that can be made with seafood or vegetables, the dish derives its name from the flat-bottomed vessel (patio) used to bhuno masalas in traditional Parsi-Gujarati households.

Unlike, say, Khichdi, Dhan Dar Patio is like three distinct notes that come together to form a perfect medley. Ask any Parsi, and you will get a whole host of suggestions for

Whether in a temple or gurudwara, the simplest of food is served to mark religious occasions. It's the same for Parsis—you'll always find Dhan Dar Patio on the menu. Why the emphasis on simple foods? For one, it means less time in the kitchen on a busy day. Two, it symbolizes our gratitude for having plain, but wholesome, food on our plates.

Ask any Parsi, and you will get a whole host of suggestions for the best way to eat Dhan Dar Patio. Me, I never use a fork and spoon; I love eating with my fingers. I think that's the best way to experience this dish.

the best way to eat it. Some people make a little hole in the middle of their rice serving and place the patio in the centre. Others prefer the occasional taste of patio on the side. Me, I never use a fork and spoon, I love eating with my fingers. I think that's the best way to experience this dish. I work my way through the serving on my plate by mixing small portions of dhan, dar and patio, ensuring that I get a taste of patio in every bite.

Recently, we did a Navroz menu for the Weekend Kitchen and offered a steel tiffin with Dhan Dar Patio along with a note explaining how to eat it. Our clients loved it!

It's astonishing how a plain arhar (tuvar) dal and rice is elevated by the addition of patio. It just changes the whole flavour when you add it. Prawn Patio is my personal favourite, and it's also the one Dolly is best known for, so I asked her to share the recipe. She seemed reluctant at first, but then I told her this funny story about the very unusual patio we created at SodaBottleOpenerWala—a Tatrelo (fried) Seafood Patio with squid, prawn and fish. I thought it was delicious, but cleary I was the only one because guests seemed to prefer the plain prawn one.

I have a feeling Dolly doesn't think much of my seafood patio either, which is why she eventually relented and shared her recipe with me!

ARUSH MOVED OUT OF HIS FAMILY home for the first time when we got married. To make the transition more comfortable for him, I began cooking Punjabi-style food with a lot of pyaaz-tamatar, adrak-lasan and hari mirch. There was Chhole and Rajma, and I made Chana Dal Tadka often too, with jeera, dried red chillies, adrak-lasan, pyaaz, tamatar and chopped dhaniya.

Punjabi households are big on beans, but my body wasn't used to such heavy fare. I found myself longing for a plain yellow pisa hua arhar dal. In that first year of marriage, I rarely made dhan dar because I thought Arush wouldn't like it.

Then one day, when I was back from a trip, I found I was done with eating heavy food. I made an Alu-Jeera sabzi and dhan dar for myself and another dal for Arush. When we sat down to eat, he wanted to know what I was having. 'You won't like this dal,' I said to him. 'It's very bland.' He had a taste, and then served himself a big bowl full of it. 'Why did you assume I wouldn't like it?' he asked, wolfing it down. Now, he loves it so much that it is made at home twice a week.

I guess I didn't imagine that something so simple can resonate with people who haven't grown up eating it, or have memories associated with it. We tend to make assumptions about people's palates without giving them a chance to make up their own minds about new flavours.

Since then, I've done several other taste experiments on Arush. I make anything that I am feeling nostalgic about, and he happily scarfs it down.

KHATTU MEETHU LOVE

A type of pyaaz-tamatar bhuna masala, there are two ingredients that give patio its distinct flavour—vinegar and sugar. It's a flavour pairing that I LOVE. I add a pinch of sugar to everything savoury. It's a very Gujarati thing, but I feel it balances the dish. Just like when you're making an Asian dressing, or a sticky sauce which has soy, chilli paste, garlic, ginger and similar ingredients, you always put either brown sugar or honey to balance the saltiness of the soy and heat of the chilli paste.

Dolly's Dhan Dar Patio

preparation time **30 mins** serves **4**

Ingredients

For the dal
1 cup arhar (tuvar) dal
1 tsp turmeric
1 tsp salt
3 cups water

For the tadka
2 tbsp ghee
1 tbsp garlic, finely chopped
1 tsp cumin seeds

For the rice
1 cup rice (any variety you like, I use Basmati)
3–4 cups water
Salt to taste
Fried onions for garnish

For the prawn
500 g prawns, shelled and deveined
1 tbsp garlic–jeera paste
1 tsp red chilli powder
1 tsp turmeric powder
1 tsp sambhar masala (p. 193)
Juice of 1 lemon | Salt to taste

For the Tomato Patio
2 large onions, finely chopped | 2 large tomatoes, finely chopped | 1 tbsp garlic, finely chopped | 2 green chillies, finely chopped | 4 tbsp oil | 1 tsp turmeric powder | ½ tsp red chilli powder | 1 tsp sambhar masala | 3 tbsp tomato puree | Salt to taste | 2 tbsp Kolah (or any other) vinegar | ½ tbsp jaggery powder/sugar | A small bunch of fresh coriander, stems and leaves separated and finely chopped | 1 tsp butter

Method

For the dal
1 In a pressure cooker, add the washed dal, salt, turmeric powder and water. Pressure cook for 3 whistles and set aside till the steam releases.
2 Remove the lid and use a dal ghotni to mash the dal.
3 For the tadka, heat ghee in a big pan. Add the cumin and then garlic, and let it lightly brown. Pour the pureed dal over the tadka and let it cook until you are happy with the consistency. It shouldn't be too thick or too thin. Check the salt, then set it aside.

For Dhan Dar, the cooked dal is completely mashed. I use a dal ghotni to get the right consistency.

For the rice

1 In a deep-bottomed pot, add water (it should be almost 3-4 times the rice), washed rice and a little salt. Let it boil, then simmer for about 20 minutes till the grains are cooked.

2 Drain the excess water and transfer the rice to an open pan or tray to cool (so that the grains don't stick).

For the patio

1 Marinate the prawn with all the ingredients and set aside for an hour.

2 In a shallow pan or kadhai, heat the oil, add the onions and fry till brown.

3 Add the ginger–garlic paste and sauté till it is light brown. Now add the green chillies and all the dry spices and cook for a few minutes.

4 Add the tomatoes, tomato puree and coriander stems. (I like adding the stems at this point because they lend an amazing aroma to the dish.) Cook till the masala comes together like a freshly made paste. Add a little water if the masala is sticking, or the tomatoes need more cooking.

4 Add the prawn and salt to taste. Cook for around four minutes.

4 Add the vinegar and jaggery. This is what makes the dish 'khattu-meethu' as the Parsis like to call it.

5 Cook for another 2 minutes, then add the butter (my secret ingredient!) and chopped coriander leaves. Patio is ready!

To serve

1 Heat the dal, and drizzle it with ghee.

2 Warm the rice and top it with lots of fried onions (birista, p 194).

3 Heat the patio.

3 Serve all three items together with fresh green chillies and onion.

PRO TIPS

I like my dal garlicky, but if you don't, reduce the amount of garlic in the tadka.

You can add 300 g fried brinjal, 500 g fish (small 35 g boneless pieces, marinated like the prawns) or 300 g roasted or boiled pumpkin for variation. You can also have a plain Tamota Nu Patio, which is delicious.

PARSI PRAWN CURRY

Mom always knows best

My mother, Nilufer, is the most instinctive cook I know. She is also one of those people who can tell you each ingredient that went into a dish she ate, maybe once, over ten years ago. I put it down to a life spent as a teetotaller!

When Kurush and I were growing up, we usually split our summers between Allahabad and Mumbai, and a huge part of those visits was spent gorging on delicious Parsi food. Fish and prawn in particular, because back then fresh seafood wasn't as easily available in Delhi as it is today. Once we came back home, Mom would try the recipes she'd eaten and liked; I recall how she'd mastered a Tibbs-style Frankie because it was a favourite of ours.

Replicating the Prawn Curry we ate on one of those trips was a tricky one. The balance of spice, the ratio of heat to coconut and the quality of prawn (only fresh please!), Mom had to get everything absolutely right. Nilufer Dhondy isn't one of those people who will make a tasty but less-than-perfect dish and be at peace with herself. She won't give up trying until she hits a flavour ten on ten. She's her own biggest critic.

I went to culinary school, worked in different hotels and restaurants, and managed a restaurant kitchen, but Mom is still the authority on everything food related. She's super organized—everything in her kitchen has a set place and you must put it back exactly where you took it from. Mom makes lists, labels everything; she may not be Le Cordon Bleu-certified, but her mise en place would put a professional chef to shame. You'll never ever catch her pulling out a bowl or fetching an ingredient mid-cook.

Raised by women who are gifted cooks, Mom has always been happiest in the kitchen. If she had gone to culinary school or run a restaurant kitchen, I've no doubt that she would have been right at the top—one of India's best

ॐ Mom's culinary expertise has been acknowledged by the family, which is why she's been entrusted with my great-grandmother Naju Mumma's masala recipes.

ॐ My love of cooking comes from Mom.

ॐ The trend of home cooks has really taken off during the pandemic, so when I think of Mom doing it back then, I realize she was ahead of her time.

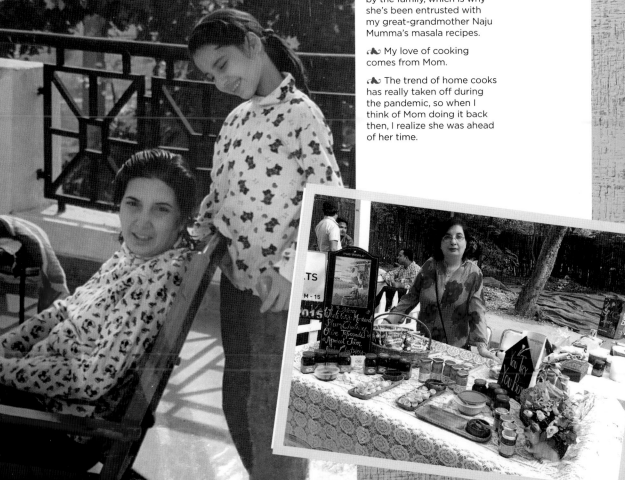

Prawn Curry is tricky. The balance of spice, the ratio of spice to coconut and the quality of prawn (only fresh please!), Mom has to get it absolutely right.

ANAHITA AND NILUFER'S WEEKEND KITCHEN

The decision to launch the Weekend Kitchen in 2020 came at time when I was going through a low phase, emotionally and physically. I felt ready to get back into the kitchen but I had to take it slow, so I thought of starting something from home. Mom was like, yeah, let's do it.

We knew we didn't want to cook all day, or take orders at just any time—that's how the idea of a weekend kitchen was born. We put up menus on Wednesdays and close orders by Thursdays. Then, we order provisions and on Friday, we prep. Saturday and Sunday mornings we cook and deliver; for the first few weeks, Arush, Dad and Kurush did the deliveries. Kurush also designed the menus, so it really is a family enterprise.

Mom and I have a very clear-cut division of responsibilities. I take care of the business part of it and we both manage the cooking. We feature a different dish every weekend and include dessert because Mom's cakes are very well known. Three months in, we've upgraded the packaging and expanded the menu beyond Parsi food. We crowdsource a lot of menu ideas, via my Instagram page—the Pulled Salli Boti Burger (right), for instance, was something we wanted to try, and my followers seconded it.

We make many traditional Parsi dishes, so I'm learning a lot too. Coming up with new dishes for our vegetarian menu and equivalents for Salli Boti and Jardalu Chicken has been one of the most fun aspects of this.

chefs, for sure. In fact, Nana offered to send her to Le Cordon Bleu (LCB) in London but Mom refused because she thought it was too expensive. Then she got married, moved to Mumbai with Dad, and had kids. Any lingering dreams of training to become a chef were shelved because she didn't want to leave us behind.

Instead, she became the perfect homemaker who honed her skills by attending workshops and cooking classes that were so popular at the time. Recently, I found her notebooks that date back thirty years or so, with handwritten recipes for Thai food, pastry, etc.

Mom loves bookmarking recipes from magazines and trying out new ideas—she rates the recipes as 'good', 'bad' and 'very good'. We've got tons of these magazines at home, because both Nani and Meher Mumma used to collect them too! Today, whenever I go to Mom's place, I flip through them. I've found some very cool recipes there.

Women at that time socialized and hosted elegant dinner parties frequently. Mom was always ahead of the game, and one dish that I still remember being fascinated by was Fish en Papillote (fish baked in parchment paper). Very old school, but I'm amazed when I think that that so much attention was given to skill, technique and presentation, and that a lot of people—mostly women—were interested in knowing more about it. Foreign food was on trend, and that's probably why Mom is puzzled by my preference for making Indian dishes. 'You went to LCB, but you don't cook any fancy food,' she points out. Mom makes Parsi dishes with flair, but she is most definitely not a dal-chawal-roti type of person. All the global cuisine you see me cooking today is inspired by Mom.

Hand-me-down recipes have been an obsession of mine, which is why Mom's masala business makes me so proud. She prepares and sells dhana-jiru and sambhar masalas from a recipe that belonged to my great-grandmother Naju Mumma—Dada's mom. When she died, we thought we had lost the recipe, until Rati Kaki (my grand-uncle Kersi's wife) shared it with Mom almost thirty-five years ago. That hand-written recipe is one of Mom's most cherished possessions.

She began making masala for the family, and later, for friends. When SodaBottleOpenerWala opened, we tested her masalas along with the other commercially available ones from Mumbai, and hers were the clear winner. Homemade, better in terms of quality, aroma, everything.

The masalas are just one example of Mom's entrepreneurial spirit. For the last thirty years, she has been catering parties across Delhi. She'd make large batches of baked dishes, salads, mayonnaise, Parsi food from scratch ... There was a time when she used to bake sixty cakes in one day, all on her own, without any help!

This trend of home cooks has really taken off during the pandemic, so when I think of her doing it back then, I realize she was ahead of her time.

MY LOVE FOR COOKING COMES from Mom; she's the one who gave me my first lessons. One of my earliest memories is of sitting on the floor of her kitchen and licking cake batter from a bowl. By the time I was twelve, I was baking cakes—I made one for Kurush's birthday and drew Superman in icing on top.

Then there was this time when I was in class three, and I had to participate in a food competition at school. Mom and I made a salad with dressing, and then she took a lauki, scooped out the insides to make a little boat, and filled it with the salad. She showed me how to make little boatmen with toothpicks, olives and cheese. Of course, I won the prize.

I was sent to cookery classes during my summer holidays, and when Mom saw how much I enjoyed being in the kitchen, she encouraged me to do more.

One of my best memories is of the two of us making chips—wafers—from scratch. We were living in Delhi's Sarvapriya Vihar at the time, and I must have been around six years old. We used a mandolin to slice the potatoes and took them up to the terrace to dry them. It was peak summer, and Mom spread the potato slices out on a bedsheet. When they became wrinkled, almost translucent, we'd store them in these big jars to be fried and tossed in masala. They were the yummiest chips—like the Hot Chips you get in Bengaluru. I remember how much fun the entire process was, though it is kind of lost now, you know? Very few people do it anymore, which is sad, because it's a great way to spend time with family.

Like our Vindaloo, Parsi Prawn Curry is a close adaptation of the Goan Curry, but with a few key differences. Goans used kokam, which gives the curry a khatas (sour flavour). Parsis, on the other hand, use poppy seeds and peanuts (the Gujarati influence). The Parsi curry also has a much heavier texture as compared to its Goan counterpart.

THE TWO OF us, well, we're quite a pair. While Mom loves to try new recipes, she's very particular about following instructions to a T. If it says, onion finely chopped, she will finely chop. She will not change the recipe. Whereas I am a person who has studied food in a very different way, created many recipes, so I experiment a lot.

Our daily squabbles are like oxygen that we breathe—it just happens, it's so natural. In most circumstances, I can be very particular about things being done my way—unless I'm doing things with Mom. I mean, I know she is the authority on it, and she will always say—I'm your mom, I know better, so I'm like haan, haan, whatever. She expects her kids to defer to her, just like she did with her parents. I don't think that happens now as much as it did when we were growing up, but she continues to expect it. That's just who she is, I guess.

After Arush and I got married, Mom is the one who set up our kitchen. Hers is a treasure trove of memories. She will pull out a serving dish or a stainless steel bartan, and proudly tell us it's from 1980, or a gift from her wedding, or anniversary, or bought when she moved to Bangalore (now Bengaluru). I've inherited the same trait and I hope that someday, my kitchen will be just like hers.

I'M STRONG BECAUSE STRONG WOMEN RAISED ME

Have you heard the saying 'stuck between a rock and a hard place'? This is a peculiar situation that women from all walks of life, across generations, face. A choice of action versus inaction, of resigning yourself to your fate or breaking free to achieve one's goals. Living the dream or making the team.

In the mid-1930s, my great-grandmother Dhun married her cousin Jamshed—to keep the bloodlines pure, it was said. Soon after, my paternal grandmother Meher was born, followed by her sister Khursheed.

An ambitious and inspired woman, Dhun was a little ahead of her time. She had both the wits and the fire to make her dream— which was to star on the silver screen—a reality. The only things holding her back were her two beautiful girls and societal expectations. Log kya kahenge ...

Tired of her warring instincts, Dhun decided it was time to act. She left her family in Allahabad and moved to Bombay, leaving Meher and Khursheed in her mother Silla Mumma's care.

The years went by, and Dhun met and fell in love with a fellow artist named Feroze Mehta. The two of them moved first to Karachi, then the Parsi Colony in the picturesque hill station of Quetta, where they took over the Lourdes Hotel and ran it all the way from the mid-1940s to the mid-1980s.

Though she changed her name to Farida Mehta, in essence, Dhun remained the same. A vivacious personality who took the opportunity to seize life. She never became famous as an artist and, in view of that, many questioned whether her decision to leave her family behind was the right one in the end.

🪶 (Left) An ambitious and inspired woman, Dhun was a little ahead of her time.

🪶 Though the age difference between them was just two years, Meher managed everything with clockwork regularity (in a recent picture with Khursheed).

🪶 Mumma (Anjul Bhandari)'s story is one of absolute true grit.

To which her daughter, my Meher Mumma, always says, 'She had a life well lived and a story to tell, which is always worth it.'

I met a woman of equal strength again when I was about to be married. Anjul Bhandari, my mother-in-law, is another Titan. Mumma's story is one of absolute true grit. Married at the young age of sixteen, she spent her early years bringing up the children. Crisis struck when she had one child in college, and the other just about to enrol. That's when Mumma, who was in her forties, decided it was time to step up. She launched her own couture label and is now on her way to becoming a market leader in fashion.

Silla Mumma, Dhun, Meher Mumma, Nani, Mom, Mumma—all these women whom I share a connection with are independent, successful and, most importantly, belong to a long line of strong women. I have never seen any of them flinch at the idea of more work or running an entrepreneurial venture. They just tackle it head on and enjoy every bit of the journey. Their legacy and success have inspired me at every step in my life.

Eight years ago, when I was hired as Chef-Manager at SBOW, I was just twenty-three and the only girl in the kitchen. There were people around me who doubted my capabilities. She is so young! Just out of culinary school and taking over our job! Bah, she's just going get married and quit the industry, they said.

It made things harder for me, but it also made me want to work extra hard, to prove that I was meant to fly.

And boy, did I soar.

Nilufer's Parsi Prawn Curry

preparation time **1 hour** serves **6**

Ingredients

500 g prawns, deveined and cleaned

For marinating the prawns
1 tsp turmeric
1 tsp red chilli powder
Salt to taste
Juice of 2 lemons

For the curry paste
2 tbsp chana, roasted
4 tbsp raw peanuts
1½ tbsp cashews, chopped
2 tsp coriander seeds
1½ tsp white sesame seeds
1½ tsp cumin seeds
1½ tsp poppy seeds
10–15 Kashmiri red chillies
10 small or 6 large garlic cloves

3 large tomatoes, roughly chopped
½ fresh coconut, grated

For the curry
4 tbsp coconut milk powder mixed with
¼ cup water
4 tsp gram flour (besan)
4 tbsp cooking oil (peanut/sesame or any
neutral oil)
1 tsp tamarind paste mixed with 2 tsp water
3 cups hot water
2 tsp red chilli powder
1 tsp turmeric powder
1½ tsp curry powder (p. 193)

For garnish
Fresh coriander, chopped
Lemon wedges

Method

1 Marinate the prawns no more than 45 minutes ahead of
   putting the ingredients together. (You don't want to do
   this too much in advance as the acid in the marinade
   will start to break down the prawn more than you want.)
   Refrigerate till 10 minutes before preparing the dish.
2 To make the curry paste, soak the Kashmiri red chillies in
   hot water. Softened, they are easier to blend.
3 Take the ingredients for the paste (chana, peanuts,
   cashews and seeds) and roast them in a pan. You can

roast each separately or together. Once they've cooled, blend them with the garlic, tomato, water and coconut till you get a nice and thick paste. If needed, do add a little water to the grinder.

3 To make the gravy, heat oil in a kadhai, add the gram flour, and roast till you get a nice nutmeg-type smell.

4 Add the curry paste to the pan and keep stirring, on medium heat, till the oil separates and the masala is fully cooked. It could take 30 minutes.

5 Add the turmeric, red chilli and curry powders, and keep stirring. Add salt to taste and then the coconut milk and water, keep stirring.

6 Let the curry boil for about 5–8 minutes till it has thickened slightly.

7 Add the prawns and keep stirring. If your prawns are small and shrimp-like, then cook for about 3–4 minutes; if they are large, cook them for about 5–7 minutes. Once the prawns are cooked, add the tamarind and cook for a few minutes on boil. Check seasoning.

8 Serve garnished with coriander and lemon wedges, along with steamed rice, potato wedges*, kachumbar and a nice crisp lager.

PRO TIPS

Fresh prawns with the shell would be the best as they would add more flavour to the curry. I get mine from Gujarat fisheries in New Delhi. You could use frozen prawns too.

I like my curry thick and with a little bit of a bite, so I add water in phases to get the consistency that I like. If you prefer it smooth, add some more water.

*To make the potato wedges, boil 2-3 large potatoes with skin. To check if they are cooked, prick with a smooth knife. Peel, and cut them into wedges while they are hot. Sauté in oil and garnish with fresh coriander.

If you don't eat prawns you could add boiled eggs!

DHANSAK

*A meal worth its
weight in gold*

THERE'S SOMETHING VERY SPECIAL about sitting down for a meal together as a family, and Dhansak on a Sunday means the world to every hardworking Parsi Daddy and his pesky bawa kids. A beautiful melange of vegetables, meat and herbs eaten with caramelized rice, kachumbar and a blaze of lemon, it's a dish best served with a rather large pint of lager, preferably Kingfisher Premium. Dhansak and beer is that big, heavy weekend meal likely to put you in a food coma. You literally need a phatka to keep your eyes open after a Dhansak lunch, so it's a good thing we can count on Mumma's constant 'don't play with your food' scolds to stay alert!

For Dhansak and me, it wasn't love at first sight. Of course, I enjoyed eating it, but I didn't ever want to learn how to make it. In my head, it was always a very complicated recipe, a belief reiterated by everyone at home (twenty-five ingredients!). Also, we're all attached to our mother's cooking so whenever I went away, I'd always want to come home and eat Mom's Dhansak.

It was while I was at Le Cordon Bleu, London, that I began thinking about Indian food in a different way. I started asking myself: Why am I running behind so many cuisines when I can do so much with my food culture? When I returned, and was at the threshold of beginning my journey with SodaBottleOpenerWala (SBOW), I went to Mom. 'Show me how you make your Dhansak. I want to make sure that we serve the recipe that I have grown up eating,' I said to her.

WHILE REDISCOVERING MY HERITAGE through food, I realized that Dhansak is a dish that mirrors my people. It's rich with inexpensive ingredients, nostalgic and full of zest, very much like my unshakeable community. The perfect medley of flavours, this recipe tells you the story of our travels, for each ingredient is a milestone covered by us.

🍂 (Clockwise from top left) Meher Mumma had the best Dhansak dinner parties.

🍂 One of the first few lunches Arush and I hosted at home.

🍂 Mom's the one who showed me how to make Dhansak, and now it's one of the most popular items on our Weekend Kitchen menu.

🍂 Meher Mumma and Beji Kaka savour the Dhansak we made at Mom's house in Gurgaon.

ANAHITA & NILUFER'S
Weekend Kitchen

Main Dishes

Veg Dhansak ₹ 550
Served with caramelised rice, kachumbar & kebabs

Mutton Dhansak ₹ 950
Served with caramelised rice, kachumbar & kebabs

Sat 8th
& Sun 9th
August 2020

Dessert

Mawa Cake ₹ 400
The popular Parsi cake which is made from mawa

EACH PORTION SERVES 2
LIMITED PORTIONS
PRE-ORDER BEFORE SELL OUT

Phone No. +91-7217817377
Please WHATSAPP on this number to place order

Fleeing religious persecution in the eighth century, Zoroastrians—followers of one of the world's oldest faiths and ideologies, based on the teachings of the prophet Zarathustra—journeyed from Iran and landed in Sanjan, Gujarat. In India, the Parsis (who came from Pars, or Fars, a small port on the coast of Persia) began familiarizing themselves with the local produce and adding new and exciting dishes to their repertoire of culinary wonders. There are many tales spun around Dhansak, but the real story lies within its name: Dhan = gold or wealth, and sak = food; it was a dish prepared with the bountiful ingredients of the new land.

Now the thing is, in Iran, there are lots of stews but also dry meats that are eaten with rice. The Indian palette, however, prefers a little curry to be eaten with roti or rice, and so the recipe evolved.

Derived from the Irani dish Khoresh, a mutton stew cooked with spinach and plums, and served with rice and mokhalafat (accompaniments) like fresh salads and herbs, pickled vegetables and flat bread, the Parsi Dhansak is much more flavourful. In layman's terms, it's dal (which was locally available) cooked together with meat and spices (they're not two separate dishes). The dal adds a lot of body and makes Dhansak a very filling dish. It has been further upgraded by adding the Basmati rice at its foundation. (Basmati, in my opinion, is the most royal of rice, compare it to any around the world!)

Except for the introduction of pumpkin, the vegetables—potatoes, onions, tomatoes, brinjal—have largely remained the same. However, the addition of coriander, mint, green chilli and methi are all Gujarati influences. The greens add a lot of freshness to this heavy dal-meat-rice preparation.

Today, whatever 'Dhansak masala' you get in the supermarket is a combination of two spices that are a staple in Parsi households: the dhana-jiru and sambhar masalas. We make our masalas at home, from a recipe passed down from my Dada's mother, Naju Mumma. She got it from her mother-in-law, possibly at the turn of the century. Mom got it from Rati Kaki, Dada's brother's wife; you know how it is between people who love to cook, they're always sharing recipes within the family. Dad's aunt only gave it to Mom because she thought Mom would do justice to it. Separately roasting each of the fifteen spices that go into the masala is a lot of hard work, but Mom is enthusiastic. She's got a badass recipe book in which she's

THE MASALA BOX

I'll let you in on a little secret—there's no such thing as Dhansak masala. That's just a convenient label. Dhana-jiru and sambhar masalas are the two pillars of Parsi food. The former is like a garam masala made up of fifteen spices; it's called dhana-jiru because dhaniya and jeera are the predominant flavours. The latter is a thecha-style, chilli-garlic masala used to marinate prawns and chicken, in patios and spicy curries.

For recipes, see p. 193.

Each of the fifteen spices that go into the masala are separately roasted, according to the recipe Mom follows. It's a lot of hard work!

You can't have a Dhansak with roti. I mean, people have leftovers but it's not the right flavour.

written all this stuff down; she even supplies the masala we use to make our Dhansak at SBOW.

Every family has its own variation of Dhansak. Some cook it with two dals, others with one; my family recipe uses four (tuvar, chana, lal masoor and kala masoor). Kala masoor is a great addition since it gives the dish a nice depth of colour and flavour. I think it's a very UP thing, if I am not wrong.

In my Nani's house in Allahabad, Dhansak is still made in an icmic cooker. Invented in 1910, this travelling cooker resembles a modern Indian tiffin (dabba) and is made up of three compartments and a container for coal at the bottom. Mutton, dal and rice for Dhansak are all placed in the dabbas in the morning, after an early breakfast, and left to cook slowly over coals until lunchtime. In four hours, everything is cooked perfectly and the Dhansak is infused with a smoky aroma.

Don't we miss the slow life? Well, we've used the cooker a couple of times when we're in the mood for slow cooking, but it is cumbersome to light the coals, etc. It's just easier to use the gas.

With the modernization of cooking techniques and cuisine, the preparation of Dhansak has evolved over the ages. The flavour of the dish, however, remains unique to every Parsi household. The dish was, and continues to be, prepared by mothers and reminds every Parsi of the warmth of their mumma's love. For me, even today, every bite brings back the memory of being home.

I was fascinated by the 'cookers of yesterday' at the Vechaar Utensils Museum in Ahmedabad.

A DEEPLY EMOTIONAL and comforting food, Dhansak is a dish that has a special significance in our lives—and deaths.

The Zoroastrian understanding of life is a full circle; we believe that every stage deserves to be celebrated. On the birth of a child, Navjote (the day a child is initiated into the Zoroastrian faith), weddings, auspicious occasions and at times to celebrate the lives of our dear departed, we enjoy a merry meal of Pulao Dal, a yakhni-style rice and meat dish, served alongside a plain dal cooked with all the vegetables. It's the same flavours as a Dhansak but prepared differently.

YES, PARSIS ARE VEGETARIAN TOO!

You've all heard the jokes about how we're a carnivorous community, but the reality is that a lot of Parsis in Gujarat are vegetarian. Meher Mumma, who is ninety-two, grew up in a vegetarian home. When she married Dada, she entered a hardcore non-vegetarian, shikaar-loving family. She started eating meat and eggs, but she also introduced them to a variety of vegetarian dishes. She was making jackfruit Dhansak long before it became fashionable! Even today, she doesn't eat meat on Tuesdays and Thursdays.

Personally, I really like vegetarian Dhansak. The jackfruit cooked in dal tastes delicious, and the fleshy texture is reminiscent of meat. It's also fine if you don't have jackfruit, since the dal itself is packed with vegetables.

This distinction is important because of the special place Dhansak occupies in our food tradition. Very few people outside our community know that this iconic dish is never served on happy occasions.

There are very few taboos in the Parsi religion. One of them is that we don't eat meat for four days after a death in the family. On the fourth day, family members break their no-meat fast with Dhansak, as it is considered a complete, nourishing meal, one that will make you feel good after the sadness and grief you've been through.

It is a celebration of the deceased's life and their legacy. It is not steeped in sorrow but a joyous feast to remember and celebrate a family member who meant so much to us. On the fourth day after my Dada passed away, we had Dhansak and beer, and played his favourite music—Jim Reeves and Dean Martin. He lived a good, long life and we wanted to honour that and celebrate it.

MY VERSION OF DHANSAK is pretty much the same as Mom's, since I follow her recipe. She's very critical about my cooking, though, and offers very specific feedback. For instance, she is not happy when I use yellow pumpkin instead of the green one in Dhansak. It's not a big difference, especially since the vegetables are mashed, but she instantly knows.

Soon after Arush and I got married, we had invited our families over for a meal. Things were going fine until I served the Dhansak.

Mom: 'There's too much pumpkin. And you have used yellow pumpkin, instead of green.'

Me: 'Oh my god, I am making it for the first time for my in-laws. Chill!'

To be honest, Arush loves my Dhansak more than Mom's. I don't actually see the difference, except mine is a bit spicier since I like to add more green chilli and sambhar masala. Maybe that's why Arush likes mine—or he could just be taking my side, you never know.

When we were doing our research for SBOW, I tried Dhansak at a lot of restaurants in Mumbai, but nothing compared to the home-cooked version of it. Adapting it for the café was very challenging because the chefs had never eaten anything like it. Unlike Butter Chicken, which they've seen, tried and know the recipe for, they didn't know what the flavour profile or texture of Dhansak was. While it was easy for them to grasp the recipe, a lot of training went into making them understand the flavours of Parsi food. I had to taste the food for two years, every single day, which was exhausting but fulfilling.

In my opinion, Dhansak is the best dish we Parsis have in our arsenal. It really connects with my kitchen philosophy, which is that food should be tasty, affordable, fresh and combine diverse ingredients.

Yes, there are Parsis who come to SBOW and say, 'My mumma's Dhansak is way better than this,' but when you're cooking multiple meals in a restaurant kitchen as opposed to preparing one dish at home, flavours are bound to change. That's why I feel that, though elaborate and complex, this quintessentially Parsi dish will continue to be a Sunday dining tradition in most bawa homes for a long time to come.

Because after you leave home, there will come a day when you realize that, although the world presents so many options, a meal cooked in your family's kitchen is the best life has to offer.

A DISH FOR EVERY OCCASION

Parsi Bhonus (feasts) have impressive spreads, whether at a seated dinner of several courses or buffet. A wedding feast—**Lagan Nu Bhonu**—kicks off with **Lagan Nu Achaar** (carrot dry fruit pickle), **Saria** (white rice papad) and a drink (Raspberry Soda is the popular choice). The mains then arrive by course—fish, chicken, meat and egg. Expect a **Saas Ni Machchi** or **Patra Ni Machchi**, followed by **Marghi Na Farcha** (a huge piece of fried chicken), **Pulao Dal** (rice-meat and dal). This is followed by an **Akuri**, either the regular kind or a **Bharuchi Akuri** (egg with dry fruits) since it's a fancy day. There's also roti, kachumbar and kebab. The meal rounds up with **Kulfi, Falooda** or **Sev**.

I had a SBOW stall at my wedding, and we served Berry Pulao and Pulao Dal; the restaurant does a special Bhonu menu through the year.

Dhansak

preparation time **1 hour** serves **2**

Ingredients

For the mutton

1 kg mutton pieces (pichla raan)

2 tbsp oil/desi ghee

2 tbsp ginger–garlic paste

4 cups water

For the dal

200 g tuvar dal

100 g chana dal

100 g lal masoor dal

50 g kala masoor dal

1 large onion, diced

1 potato, diced

2 tomatoes, diced

80 g brinjal, peeled and diced

80 g green pumpkin, peeled and diced

4–5 tbsp coriander leaves with stem, roughly chopped

3–4 mint stalks and leaves

1 tbsp ginger–garlic paste

15–20 curry leaves

1½ tbsp fenugreek leaves (fresh or dried)

5–6 green chillies

3 tsp sambhar masala (p. 193)

2 tsp dhana-jiru masala (p. 193)

2 tsp red chilli powder

1 tsp turmeric powder

1 tsp cumin powder

1 tsp garam masala (optional)

4 cups of mutton stock

2 cups water

Salt to taste

For the caramelized rice

4 tbsp sugar

2 cups long-grained rice

1–2 green cardamoms

1–2 cloves

1–2 bay leaves

1–2 small cinnamon sticks

1 tsp cumin seeds

2 tsp salt

3 tbsp desi ghee/oil

4 cups water

For the kachumbar

4 medium-sized onions

4 medium-sized tomatoes

1 large cucumber

Salt to taste

6 tbsp lemon juice

3–4 green chillies

A handful of coriander leaves

For the kababs

500 g chicken mince

1 onion, finely chopped

2 green chillies, finely chopped

A bunch of coriander, finely chopped

2 medium-sized potatoes, boiled and grated

½ tsp turmeric powder

½ tsp red chilli powder

1 tsp sambhar masala

1 tsp dhana-jiru or garam masala

1 tbsp ginger–garlic paste

1 slice of bread
1 egg
Salt and pepper
to taste
200 g suji

Oil for frying

For garnish
4 onions, finely sliced and
deep fried (birista p. 194)

Method

For the mutton
1 Heat the oil or ghee in a pressure cooker. (It's always better to make the meat with ghee.)
2 Add the ginger–garlic paste and mutton pieces, and bhuno (fry).
3 Once the pieces are browned, add water and let the mutton cook with the lid on a slow flame. Give it at least 4 whistles followed by an additional 15-20 minutes. Check if the meat is cooked, then remove the mutton pieces and keep aside.
4 Strain the stock and use it to cook the dal. This flavour is what completes the connection between the dal and the mutton; this is the bridge.

For the dal
1 In the same pressure cooker, combine all the ingredients for the dal and the stock from the mutton and bring to a boil.
2 Cook for 3 whistles followed by 15 minutes on simmer. The consistency should be that of a thick dal with vegetables.
3 Cool and blend (or process through a food mill).

For the rice
1 Add the oil and sugar in a pan over low heat.
2 Once the sugar has caramelized (and is a light brown colour), add all the whole spices, rice and water. Add salt to taste.
3 Bring it to a boil, simmer, and cook till done.

For the kachumbar

1 Finely chop the onions, tomatoes, cucumbers, green chillies, and coriander leaves.
2 Transfer the kachumbar to a pretty glass bowl and chill in the refrigerator. Add salt and lemon juice just before serving.

For the kababs

1 Strain any excess water from the chicken mince.
2 In a bowl, mix the mince with onion, green chillies, coriander, and potato.
3 Add all the dry masalas and ginger–garlic paste.
4 Dip the slice of bread in a bowl of water, squeeze it dry and crumble into the potato mixture.
5 Add salt, pepper, and an egg. Mix well.
6 Shape the mince into balls (I make mine about 30 g each) and roll in the suji. Deep fry, shallow fry or air fry till golden brown. Makes 20 kababs.

Assembling the Dhansak

1 Mix the mutton pieces with the dal, and check the seasoning.
2 Heat the dal and mutton and let it boil for around 15 minutes until it all comes together beautifully.
3 Fluff up the rice, arrange the kababs around it and garnish with fried onions.
4 Place the chilled bowl of kachumbar on the table.
5 Put the mutton-dal in the centre of the table, with a big ladle.
6 And lastly, some chilled bottles of beer to wash it all down. Cheers!

PRO TIPS

The pichla raan (back leg) is the most tender cut. Be sure to use a leg with the bone in.

Make the dal a day ahead; the flavours kind of come together and your Dhansak will taste even better.

The kachumbar brings a brand new texture to the dish and hence is a very important element on your plate.

For the kababs, you can swap the chicken mince with mutton kheema or even soya granules or potato.

Make vegetarian Dhansak by leaving out the mutton and using water instead of stock to cook the dal.

PAV
Bombay meri jaan

AN HOMAGE TO THE DYING LEGACY of the bustling, quirky and real-world Bombay Irani Cafe? SodaBottleOpenerWala (SBOW). On paper it was an ambitious idea back in 2013 but full credit to AD Singh for his vision, and to the creative talents of Chef Sabyasachi (Saby) Gorai and Sabina Singh who brought it together. I came in a month before they opened; they wanted someone with a culinary background, but also a Parsi face for the restaurant. I had just returned to India after my LCB course and fit the bill so I was appointed Chef-Manager.

Pav featured in a starring role on the menu. We tried several recipes before the restaurant opening but none of them worked. We even flew in fresh Ladi Pav from Mumbai. Good pav, when pressed in the centre with your finger, springs back, and has a nice golden-brown colour, with a slightly chewy texture, on top. For this, getting the baking temperature right was essential.

After multiple trials, and thanks to the combined expertise of our excellent bakers Yunis and Shivaji, we found a recipe that gave us pav that was fluffy, risen to the perfect height and with a chewy, golden top. Not to toot my own horn but I have tried pav almost everywhere in Delhi, and not found an equal to the one we make at SBOW.

The Nankhatai at SBOW is inspired by a 100-year-old recipe.

CONTRARY TO POPULAR BELIEF, Ladi Pav is not an Irani bakery creation. This softer, chewier bread came to Mumbai via Goa, where it was introduced by the Portuguese who missed their native bread. The challenge they faced was having to bake bread without yeast, which wasn't locally available. In her book *Curry: A Tale of Cooks and Conquerors*, food historian Lizzie Collingham tells us that the settlers' Goan cooks resolved that problem by using toddy to ferment the dough. When these Goan cooks migrated to Bombay (now Mumbai), many became bread-makers and went on to popularize the Portuguese 'Pao' in the shape and size we know today.

It's called 'Ladi Pav' because the pav is arranged in slabs, or ladis.

Pav is baked by both Goan and Irani bakers. Soon, it was served as a side to many soupy dishes, from Misal to Vindaloo to Salli Boti. And it became a staple in Mumbai homes. I recall how, on visits to Kemps Corner during my childhood, we would eagerly await the pavwalla who delivered fresh pav door-to-door daily. Parsis love pav, and it complements our food perfectly. Just imagine yourself breaking a piece of pav, dunking it into a fragrant, spicy bowl of kheema and letting it soak up all the gravy. Unlike, say, sliced bread, pav is made in such a way that the gluten expands, giving it a very, very spongy and soft texture.

At home, I like to bake fresh pav when I'm making Kid Gosht (p. 177), Pork Vindaloo, a stew or even Moussaka. Baking it yourself can take up to four hours or so, but honestly, if you don't have the time, or the inclination to do so, store-bought pav is great too. Just one tip—unlike the Mumbai pav, which is soft, fresh and can be eaten as is, the pav in Delhi is quite dense and heavy. What I do is cut one pav into three parts and warm it on the tava with a little bit of butter and oil. Toasting it makes it easier to digest.

Parsis love pav and it complements our food perfectly. Just imagine yourself breaking a piece of pav, dunking it into a fragrant, spicy bowl of kheema ...

THE BEST TIME OF THE DAY at SBOW is the bread-making ritual. We bake fresh pav—200, 300, even 400 pieces—a day, and obviously we don't do it by hand. We have a huge commercial machine to make the dough, which is then proofed for an hour. The dough is then rolled out—it takes three people!—shaped into balls and baked.

Now, the timing of the rolling of the dough is crucial because it must be done quickly. Remember, we are not talking a small 100 g ball in a bowl. There are probably 10 kilos of dough, a huge amount. It is a community exercise, with the team standing at the table, rolling dough, chatting about their day. It's a time when we discuss the issues someone may be facing, gossip or just talk about what is going on in each of our lives. Mind you, this is at 5 a.m., which is when the bakery team comes into work.

Once the tray of pav goes into the oven, it's baked for ten minutes, pulled out, turned, and slid back in. What this does is give the pav an even brown colour on top. As soon as the pav is taken out, we brush it with a mixture of oil and butter. After that, the entire tray is turned upside down and the pav is cooled, face down, on a wire rack for about five minutes before it is turned. This last step is important as it prevents the pav from becoming mouldy.

The entire process takes about six hours—after proofing the rolled dough, it bakes quickly, in fifteen minutes or so. During this time, we have our morning chai and leftover pav heated in the oven with a little butter. We sit, relax and joke about having to be back on our feet soon.

I may have bid adieu to SBOW, but I will always cherish those memories of chai time with my wonderful team.

Pav

preparation time **4 hours** serves **8**

Ingredients

600 g flour	1 egg
10 g instant yeast	200 ml milk, slightly warmed
80 g sugar	150 ml cream
6 g salt	Butter/oil for glazing

Method

1 Mix sugar, yeast and milk in a large bowl. Keep aside for 5 minutes till the yeast blooms.

2 Now add all the remaining ingredients, except the salt, to the yeast mixture. Knead for 5–8 minutes and then add the salt. (The kneading is through stretch and fold, if using your hands. Otherwise, you can use a food processor.)

3 Knead the dough till the windowpane test* is successful.

4 Leave the dough to prove/rise in a bowl dusted with flour (or greased with oil) and cover with a wet towel.

5 After about an hour, the dough will have doubled. Poke it and gently knock out the air. Divide the dough into equal parts—50 g each for pav and 80 g for buns.

6 Grease an oven-safe tray with butter or oil.

7 Roll the dough balls and lay them out proportionately.

8 Cover the dough balls with a wet cloth for another 30–45 minutes, allowing them to rise again.

9 Preheat your oven to 180°C. Reduce the temperature to 170°C and bake the pav for 20 minutes and then at 180°C for 10 minutes.

10 Remove the tray from the oven and transfer the pav to a cooling rack. Glaze with butter/oil to keep them soft.

PRO TIP

For the windowpane test—take a piece of dough, about the size of a golf ball, and hold it between your thumb and first two fingers. If you can stretch the dough into a thin translucent square (i.e. a windowpane) without it breaking, your dough is ready to rise.

MUTTON BERRY PULAO

OTHER THAN PAV, if there is one Bombay special that I poured my heart and soul into perfecting, it is Berry Pulao. I've lost count of the number of DMs I've received on Instagram for the recipe. I couldn't do this book without including it!

Ironically, there is no such thing as Berry Pulao in Iran. I read an article on how Iranis use zereshk, or barberry, in their food. A tiny, sour-tasting red berry, it's difficult to get in India. They also use a lot of dry fruits, raisins and dates in their rice preparations.

Then where and how did Berry Pulao originate? In a small but majestic corner café in Ballard Pier called Britannia & Co, which has been one of the greatest inspirations for SBOW. Legend has it that Berry Pulao was created by the late Boman Kohinoor's wife. I have visited the place many times with my family, and always enjoyed the Berry Pulao.

If I had to describe it, I'd say it was made with shredded meats in flavourful saffron rice. At SBOW, we tried everything to get the flavours of our Berry Pulao on point. I even tried charming the recipe out of Boman Uncle and got a scolding for it. 'Sit down and eat your Lagan Nu Custard and don't ask too

many questions,' he said. It's unfortunate that people are so possessive. So many important recipes have been lost because of this!

Eventually though, SBOW chefs Kulbir and Pratap perfected the Berry Pulao recipe under Saby's guidance. Inspired by Britannia, it has evolved slightly over time. For starters, the Berry Pulao at Britannia is much drier than the one we make. Our mutton, slowly braised with spices, has a slight gravy that is absorbed by our beautiful golden rice, which is Basmati flavoured with sugar, saffron milk, spices and salt.

INGREDIENTS

For the mutton mixture
1 kg mutton (with bone)
2 tbsp ginger–garlic paste
2 onions, sliced
1 tsp red chilli powder
1 tsp coriander powder
Salt to taste
1–2 pieces of star anise
1–2 medium-size cinnamon sticks
1–2 bay leaves
4 tbsp oil

For the masala
2 onions, chopped
2 tomatoes, chopped
3–4 tbsp oil
1–2 green chillies, finely chopped
4 tbsp tomato puree
Salt to taste
1 tsp red chilli powder
1 tsp sambhar masala
1 tsp turmeric powder
1 tsp coriander powder
1 tsp cumin powder
1–2 tbsp chopped coriander

For the rice
1 cup Basmati rice
5–6 cups of water
Salt to taste
5 tbsp sugar
1–2 pieces of star anise
1–2 medium-size cinnamon
1–2 bay leaves
3–4 cloves
4–5 green cardamoms
3 tbsp desi ghee
5–6 strands of saffron mixed with ½ cup of warm milk

To garnish
Fried cashewnuts
Fried onions
Fried berries (barberries or Iranian zereshk berries; you could also use cranberries or blackcurrents)
Coriander and mint leaves

METHOD

For the mutton
1 Heat oil in a pressure cooker and add the whole spices.
2 Add the onions and sauté. Then, add the ginger–garlic paste and then the mutton. Bhuno well.
3 Add the powdered spices, salt and water (just enough to cover the mutton) and pressure cook for 4 whistles and 15 minutes on simmer. Once cooked, remove the meat pieces. Reserve the stock.

For the masala
1 Heat oil in a pan, add the onions and sauté till brown. Now add green chillies, all powdered spices and cook for another 12 minutes. Add tomato puree and mix.
2 Add the tomatoes and let the mixture boil and become thick.
3 Add the mutton stock and let it come to a boil. Then add the mutton pieces and let it cook until the meat has absorbed the gravy. Set it aside.

For the rice
1 Wash the rice a few times and leave it to soak for about 30 minutes, then drain.
2 In a large pot over medium heat, add the water, salt, sugar and whole spices.
3 Add the rice to the pot, cook till it comes to a rolling boil and let it simmer. Once the rice is ready (around 15 minutes), drain the excess water. Add the ghee and saffron milk and cover.

To serve
Scoop the rice into a bowl. Place the mutton pieces and some masala in the centre and top with more rice. Demould the rice on to a platter and garnish.

Note Add blanched veggies (beans, carrots), fried potatoes and cauliflower to the masala for a vegetarian version.

FRIED BOOMLA

*On the road to
discovering my roots*

WHEN I BEGAN JOTTING down ideas for this book, I realized that while I wanted to share stories about my family, I also wanted to discover some new things about my culinary roots. Dishes that I had never tasted, places that had remained undiscovered; I wanted to know more about where my cuisine originated. And all signs pointed to Gujarat.

By then, I'd been working at SodaBottleOpenerWala (SBOW) for almost three years and cooking tons of Parsi food. But I'd ask myself: am I on the right path? It seemed like I was—from the people I consulted, books I read and the feedback that I received. Now, I needed to go back to where it had all begun and challenge my tastebuds, see if I really was doing a good job or just bullshitting my way through.

I reached out to Dr Shernaz Cama, director of the UNESCO Parzor Project for the Preservation and Promotion of Parsi Zoroastrian Culture and Heritage, and she connected me to Mr Dinshaw Tamboly, chairman of the World Zoroastrian Organisation (WZO) Trusts in India. He was very sweet and helped plan my road trip to Sanjan, Navsari and Udvada in November 2016.

Oh, and I did it on my own—no mother, father or brother for company … and I genuinely loved having so much time to myself. It was the best trip.

SANJAN

To commemorate the day our ancestors arrived on the coast of Gujarat, the Parsis organize a Sanjan jashan (thanksgiving ceremony). I arrived just in time to participate in the festivities. The jashan is performed by the priests of Udvada at the Sanjan Stambh, a memorial column built in 1917. Stalls are set up to mark the occasion, and I bought chalk (Parsi rangoli), spices and chavanu, a type of chakhna made with puffed or flattened rice, chana dal, dry spices, etc.

🐚 (Top) The Atash Behram in Navsari is over 250 years old.

🐚 (Left) The Sanjan Stambh commemorates the arrival of the Zoroastrians in India in the year 936. The column was built in 1920 to honour this memory.

I had the privilege of sampling two types of Falooda's—mango and kesar—at the Yazdan Cold Drink House in Navsari. Ask me which one I liked better? I couldn't choose! Both are absolutely delish!

Never imagined I would learn how to make Chokha Ni Rotli (rice flour rotli) on a lakra no choolo (wood-fired stove) in a village a few kilometres from Navsari.

Sanjan is such a small, sparsely populated town, that you go left from the stambh to the agiary and right to the market. That's it. The town is over. Small but lovely. It was truly an enriching experience.

NAVSARI

Mr Dinshaw Tamboly had insisted that I visit Navsari and see the WZO Senior Citizens Centre. Okay, I said, but wondered, what am I going to learn there? How will it help me build my culinary repertoire?

Once I reached, to my surprise, I spent two days in the kitchen where they cooked meals for the residents. Honestly, I was very touched to see how well Parsis take care of their community. I stayed in the old people's home for two nights, and passed my time chatting and playing chess and Scrabble with them. The kitchen was huge and very old school. It reminded me of my grandmother's kitchen because all the cutting, chopping, etc., was done sitting on the ground. Even the rotis and rotlas were all rolled out on a chakla on the floor. The food was homely and simple, but delicious—Lapsi (broken wheat porridge) for breakfast, dhan dar and fried fish or a Pulao Dal for lunch, and rotli and meat stew for dinner. I especially enjoyed the Papri Ma Gosht, meat cooked with a broad, flat bean. A very Parsi thing to get people to eat vegetables by adding meat to the dish!

I also spent half a day at First Dastoor Meherjirana Library, one of the oldest repositories of books in the world and home to several ancient Parsi texts. I also visited the Kolah factory to see how their famous vinegar is made.

Other memorable eats in Navsari were the Faloodas at Yazdan Cold Drink House—where you'll find unusual flavours like gulkand and kaju draksh—and Kolaji Famous Falooda. I also had the best Bhakras—a sweet donut made of maida. It's a snack that goes excellently with chai.

UDVADA

A sleepy, tiny town on the coast of Gujarat, Udvada is the Char Dham equivalent for Parsis. I was nine when I first visited the Iranshah Atash

Behram. It was after my Navjote, and I was there to page paro (seek blessings) and express my gratitude at having been embraced by the Zoroastrian faith.

Udvada is home to nine priestly families who tend to the consecrated fire, and on this visit, I made friends with two of the Dasturji boys. They took me to the agiary at night, which was such a unique experience. Praying in a room lit only by a flame, surrounded by the warm fragrance of sandalwood, was so peaceful and meditative. It's sad that non-Parsis cannot enter this sacred space because of a promise made so many years ago.

While I visited the Iranshah every day, I also wanted to experience the other attractions the town had to offer. I was staying at the Globe Hotel, run

FINDING FRENY

A year before my Gujarat road trip, in 2015, my parents and I visited Freny Ginwalla in Ahmedabad. Freny is Nana's cousin's cousin, and someone with a vast collection of heirloom recipes. We spent a lovely afternoon going through her cookbook collection and talking about Parsi cuisine and culture. At ninety-plus, Freny Aunty is happiest cooking for guests, and we thoroughly enjoyed the Patra Ni Machchi, Caramel Custard and other Parsi delights she prepared for us. In fact, she's the one who showed me how you can use butter paper if you don't have banana leaves for Patra Ni Machchi! It's the kind of homespun advice that I wanted to incorporate in my book.

🫚 (Left) Doodh Na Puff is not as difficult to make as they say it is. For my Lost Recipes pop-up at SBOW, I used a hand blender to create the jhaag.

🫚 Hand-churned fresh fruit ice cream from a guy on a cycle was my favourite dessert.

There's a bounty of Bombay duck in Udvada. Fresh fish is delivered door-to-door daily and the excess catch is dried and sold.

(Below) At SBOW's Lost Recipes Chef's Table, Fried Boomla, Aleti Paleti and Malido were some of the dishes I recreated.

THE PARSI KITCHEN 153

by a very nice couple named Percy and Zubina Sidhwa. It's where I tasted a fish called boi (mullet) for the first time. Considered a delicacy, it's a fish with lots of little teeth and not to everyone's taste.

The other dish I rediscovered was Doodh Na Puff, which is similar to Makhan Malai or Daulat Ki Chaat. I had heard my great-grandmother used to make it in winter. She would boil milk and sugar and leave it outside, uncovered, all night. It is said that the dew or frost helped chill/set the milk and, in the morning, she would use a wooden churner to froth it up. Drizzled with rose water and topped with nuts, the drink was served for breakfast.

I never had my great-grandmother's version, but the one lady in Udvada who makes it brought me a freshly churned glass, knocking on my hotel room door at 7 a.m. to serve it. It tastes like you have clouds in your mouth. A deliciously comforting concoction of sweet milk with a hint of rose water, it was also quite heavy. I went back to sleep immediately!

It was on my walk to the Doodh Na Puff lady's home that I chanced upon a miraculous sight. Rows and rows of my absolute favourite fish—Bombay duck.

PARSIS ARE BONKERS ABOUT Bombay duck. Some like their boomla dried (sukha), others prefer it fresh. Me, I'm definitely in the latter category.

On every trip to Mumbai, this is literally all I want to eat. It is so tasty, and just melts in your mouth.

Two things you need to know about Bombay duck. One, it's best eaten fried because it's a fish rich in Omega-3. (It also contains a lot of water.) Two, it looks scary as hell. Cleaning it is a task best given to someone you want to torture—how ironic then, that when we served it at our Lost Recipes pop-up at SBOW Delhi, I cleaned the whole lot myself!

Coming from Delhi, where fresh Bombay duck is hard to find, I was shocked at the amount of fish I saw in Udvada. The catch is usually so large, that the fisherfolk have no choice but to dry it. Strong and pungent, sukha boomla is an acquired taste that I've just not been able to gain.

Luckily, there was plenty of fresh boomla available as well and I had it with every meal during my stay in Udvada.

Fried Boomla

preparation time **1 hour** serves **4**

Ingredients

½ kg fresh Bombay duck

For marinating the fish
½ tsp turmeric powder
1 tsp red chilli powder
Juice of 2 lemons
1 tsp salt

For the coating
5 tbsp rice flour
2 tbsp semolina
Oil for shallow/deep frying
(depending on
what you want)

For the chutney
See chutney recipe on p. 89

Method

1 Clean and wash the Bombay duck. Remove the fin and tail and wash the gut thoroughly.
2 In a tray, lay them on paper and squeeze out the excess water*.
3 In a bowl, mix all the ingredients for the marination.
4 Add the fish and marinate it well.
5 Mix the rice flour and semolina in a plate or tray.
6 When ready to eat, coat the fish with the mixture and fry. This cooks quickly so about 3–4 minutes in hot oil is enough. Serve fresh, with green coconut chutney or lemon, which is the classic pairing!

PRO TIP

*To clean the fish, remove head, tail and gills. Make a slit in the gut and run the fish under cold water. Pat it dry and place it on a tray on paper towels. Put something heavy on top of the fish until the excess water is all squeezed out. If you just wash, dry, coat and fry, the fish will crumble.

KHARA
BHEEDA

*Soulmates meet
at Sarvapriya Vihar*

Do I believe in a supreme power? Let's just say there are days when I think we could all use a little bit of divine help. However, based on my own experience, it is my firm conviction that life is cyclical. What goes around does indeed come around.

Call it karma or coincidence, this is an extraordinary story.

My parents are true-blue, bonafide Parsis. The promise given by the Parsi people, when they first landed in India, eventually led to certain restrictions such as being penalized for marrying outside the community. It's a rule that is taken very seriously till date by Parsis living in certain parts of the country. My parents were raised with those beliefs; they fell in love at a very young age and eventually married.

Dad, an ad man, moved cities for his career—from Allahabad to Delhi, Bengaluru, Mumbai and finally New Delhi, where my parents set up home in a south Delhi colony back in 1989. Even today, 3/7 Sarvapriya Vihar remains a fantastic location, with a beautiful view of Bijay Mandal, an ancient protected monument, and its lush green surroundings.

My parents, who are very sociable people, made friendships that would last more than a lifetime in Sarvapriya Vihar. Despite having most of their immediate family in Allahabad and Mumbai, they really felt at home here. We were one big joint family. I went across to the Chanders' house to play or to study with the Lals. Soon, the Kodesias joined, and then came the Bajajs. It was in this corner house, filled with camaraderie and joy, that my parents began a new chapter in their lives.

All the love notwithstanding, there were occasional spats between neighbours. One of the most memorable incidents involved a guard named Bahadur, employed by Mr Deb who lived on the ground floor of our house. When Bahadur's job was terminated, Dad gave him shelter by offering him the house-help room on the terrace.

When Arush and I moved in, the bounty from my favourite kafir lime tree (left) was as plentiful as I recalled from my childhood days.

Marriage is a journey, and it is amazing to think that my parents, and Arush and I started out from the same location. Could there be a better omen?

#PUNJUBAWI'S HAPPILY EVER AFTER

When Arush and I were planning our wedding, we wanted to acknowledge that it was the coming together of two very distinct cultures. Punjabis are so OTT, while Parsis are much more subtle. But there are many similarities between our communities too. Food, drink and laughter are integral to us both. That's how #PunjuBawi came about. Everyone called me 'bawi', but this became our wedding hashtag, and I've used been using it ever since.

Dad drove a 1959 Bat-Wing Fiat back then. When he'd go to Siri Fort to play tennis, he would have Bahadur in tow, who would clean the car (and try his hand at a game or two!). If Dad asked him about the scratches and dents, Bahadur made a convincing case for their being Dad's fault. This carried on for some time, until Dad finally called him out on it. He insisted Bahadur take a 'driving test'.

Bahadur zoomed the car in reverse and parked it perfectly without a mistake or a scratch. Dad was shocked and asked Bahadur to turn the car again, so it would be ready for him to drive to work. As soon as Bahadur put the car in first gear, he let the clutch go. Dad stood there, watching as the car hurtled towards Mrs Lal's house, smashing a part of the boundary wall.

A shaken Bahadur emerged, unhurt. 'I am sorry,' he told Dad. 'I only know how to reverse. I can't drive forward.'

Mrs Lal complained, and Bahadur nearly found himself out of a job. On hearing this, Dad promptly hired him and gave him ten days of proper driving lessons. The rest is history as Bahadur is still with the family thirty-two years to the date.

Dad's magnanimous gesture created ripples in the peaceful haven that was Sarvapriya Vihar. To appease Mrs Lal, Dad transplanted a kafir lime tree that she admired greatly from our garden to her front yard. Mrs Lal was happy, but I was mad. It was my favourite tree, and Dad just gave it away. I remember crying, and him telling me some existential spiel that I had no understanding of at the time.

'Nothing is really ours to give or someone else's to take ... it is always and never ours forever.'

BY 1995, MY PARENTS WERE ready to buy a home of their own. As much as they loved Sarvapriya Vihar, they couldn't afford a house in south Delhi and they would have to settle for a flat! Dad took the decision to move to Gurgaon, and that's where I was raised.

In 2004, I met Arush Bhandari, a fat funny guy. He was a little bit of a bully, but smooth as butter and he could talk his way out of a storm. We became friends and eventually I fell in love. Him being a ghee-blooded Punjabi,

I thought my parents would never accept our relationship. However, I took the plunge, ready with my plan B—which was to run away—in case things went downhill. I asked Dad if Arush could come and see him. 'As soon as possible,' Dad said. Not a response I was expecting!

Three days later, twenty-seven-year-old Arush shows up at our house in his loudest Louis Vuitton shoes, whitest Armani shirt and glitzy Ferragamo belt with a bouquet of flowers in one hand and a bottle of Glenfiddich 15 Solera Reserve in the other. You can't get more Delhi than that!

The whiskey was clearly a winner with Dad and, after drinks, he and Arush had an hour-long private conversation which I have no knowledge of, till date. All I know is that a few months later, Arush and I got engaged.

Now, Arush Bhandari is a mumma's boy through and through. Street gangster home puppy ... you know the type. He's never experienced living alone for extended periods of time like I have. However, when we were about to get married, he suddenly decided that he wanted to move out into a home of his own. For the next four months, as I organized the wedding, Arush looked for apartments to rent in New Delhi. Greater Kailash, Safdarjung, Som Vihar, R.K. Puram, Green Park, Vasant Kunj ... he saw over fifty places in two months. Too expensive, not Vaastu enough, poorly lit, too hot—nothing hit that sweet spot.

Then one day, Arush and I were at my parents' place in Gurgaon when our old neighbour dropped in. Arush was introduced to Dhiraj Uncle, and somehow the conversation veered towards our house hunt. Dhiraj Uncle asked us over to his house the following weekend. Bahadur, who had mastered the art of driving forward by now, drove us there.

It had been so many years since I had visited Sarvapriya Vihar, I had forgotten the smell of my favourite kafir lime tree now planted in Mrs Lal's yard. Imagine how utterly astonished I was when Dhiraj Uncle took us to his ground floor apartment at 3/8 Sarvapriya Vihar. The apartment he had in mind was right opposite the house where I was born!

Arush and I saw the place and instantly fell in love. We took it immediately and moved in after we got married.

In those blissful early days, whenever I'd catch a whiff of tangy kafir lime, I remembered Dad's wise words. 'Nothing is really ours to give or someone else's to take … it is always and never ours forever.' Finally, I understood. Life always comes full circle.

THERE ARE TIMES WHEN I'VE ASKED Arush, who do you love more—food or me? His answer? Food!

Our marriage consists of moments when we've found ourselves outside of our comfort zone, in places where we've travelled to eat and experience the local culture. On our honeymoon, we went to Marché des Enfants Rouges, the oldest market in France. It was almost closed, but we bought a beer, a baguette and some cheese, and had the most amazing sandwich meal together. I love that no matter what I want to try out, Arush's always up for it.

Why would I pick Khara Bheeda as the preparation closest to our hearts? Well, for starters, we both love bhindi. I seem to remember eating a lot of it during our first year of marriage. Arush never thought I would cook for him—he thought I was too much of a hoity-toity chef to cook ghar ka khana. But, we had no house help, so I made everything from chapatti and rice to dal and sabzi. It was a first for me, and there was a certain charm to it that I wouldn't trade for the world.

Arush thought I was too much of a
hoity-toity chef to cook ghar ka khana.

Khara Bheeda

preparation time **20 mins** serves **4**

Ingredients

500 g bhindi, washed, tops and bottoms removed and cut into small pieces

2 onions, finely sliced

2–3 tbsp oil (sesame/peanut/ sunflower) or ghee

1 tsp cumin seeds

1–2 green chillies, chopped

1 tbsp ginger–garlic paste

1 tsp turmeric powder

1 tsp red chilli powder

1 tsp sambhar masala (p. 193)

2 tomatoes, finely chopped

Salt to taste

Method

1 Heat the oil in a pan and add the cumin seeds and onions. Fry till the onions are transluscent.

2 Add the green chillies and ginger–garlic paste. Sauté well.

3 Add the dry masalas and bhindi. Mix well for a few minutes.

4 Add the tomatoes and salt before the bhindi starts getting sticky. Don't add any water, just put a lid on it and let it cook for 5–10 minutes. Enjoy hot with rotli or parathas.

PRO TIP

If you want a crisp, dry sabzi, wash and dry the bhindi a few hours before chopping and cooking. It prevents the bhindi from becoming sticky as it cooks.

The Future

I HAVE ALWAYS BEEN a big advocate for repurposing food—it's something that I learnt ages ago from Mom. I've seen her use leftovers to make fried rice; a crumble with apples on the verge of going bad, gulgulas or banana bread, which I love, from overripe bananas. Any excess fruit was turned into jam and chutneys in our house.

Three years into running SodaBottleOpenerWala (SBOW), I realized that there was a lot more we could be doing with the ingredients that went into the bin. I took time out to focus on this and came up with a sustainable practices plan. One of my goals was putting biodiversity on our menu.

The SBOW menu already highlighted local, indigenous and seasonal foods, so I decided to focus on reintroducing traditional ingredients. With support from The Earth Collective's Meenu Nageshwaran and Pallavi Upadhyaya of Millets for Health, I added millets on the menu at SBOW. While Pallavi taught me the basics of how to cook them, I concentrated on creating dishes that would change the perception of millets as 'boring' and create a demand for this nutritious, low-water-consuming ancient grain (see recipe on p. 172).

The SBOW millets menu was a first-of-its-kind, and got people talking on social media. Food columnist Sourish Bhattacharyya and Tasting India founder Sanjoo Malhotra introduced me to Paul Newnham, director of the Sustainable Development Goal (SDG) 2 Advocacy Hub. At the time, Paul was setting up the Chefs' Manifesto, a community of global chefs advocating for a better food future, one 'where ingredients are grown with respect for the environment, where no good food goes to waste and where everyone, everywhere enjoys the nutritious meals they need to grow and thrive.' Paul saw the work I was doing at SBOW with millets and invited me to be a part

In Stockholm, I made canapes with expired groceries.

of the launch at the EAT Stockholm Food Forum in 2018. I was one of the thirteen people from all over the world to launch this initiative, and the only one from India. It was such an honour to be on a panel with Dr David Nabarro, former Special Adviser to the UN for Sustainable Development and Climate Change.

Today, this network boasts over 800+ chefs from across 77 countries. I now travel the world, advocating the benefits of Indian ingredients, especially millets. They are good for the planet as they require less water to grow, unlike rice or wheat. They are healthy, highly nutritious and gluten-free. Most importantly, they are grown all over India. The Indian government has declared 2023 as Year of the Millet, and it makes me so happy that this conversation I have been wanting to have for the past six years will finally be a part of the mainstream. Hopefully, this initiative will lead to a rise in millet sales which will not only bring about a long-lasting positive change for our farmers but also on our eating habits for generations to come.

UP UNTIL FIVE YEARS ago, the word chef wasn't cool. An interest in a culinary arts career was often looked down upon, considered the last resort for students after class twelve. If you weren't good at anything, you got into hospitality!

It's only with the rise of social media and growing awareness about our profession that things are changing. Chefs now have a new platform for self-expression; it's almost like putting your personality on a plate.

Over the years, I've been approached by many parents wanting to know if this a sound career choice for their kids. I always tell them, it's an exciting space to be in today and there are lots of options. I'm so thankful I was given the opportunity to chase my dreams. I can't wait to see what happens next!

RECIPES

Some of my all-time favourites

Falooda

preparation time **30 minutes** serves **4**

INGREDIENTS

1 tbsp sabja (sweet basil) seeds
½ cup warm water
3 tbsp vermicelli (falooda sev)
1 cup water
2 cups chilled milk
4 tbsp rose syrup
2 tbsp rose water
4 scoops vanilla ice cream
10–12 cubes of ice

METHOD

1 Soak the sabja seeds in warm water for 30 minutes till they bloom.
2 Boil the 1 cup water in a pan, cook the vermicelli and keep aside. (Ensure the sabja and vermicelli are cool or chilled before assembling.)
3 Take the ice cubes in a jug. Add the milk, rose syrup and rose water. Stir well.
4 To assemble the falooda: layer the vermicelli at the bottom of a glass, add a drizzle of rose syrup; pour the flavoured milk and top with sabja seeds. Top the glass with a scoop of vanilla ice cream. Serve chilled!

Rainbow Millet Salad

preparation time **45 minutes** serves **4**

INGREDIENTS

For the millets
100 g kodo millets (you
can also use buckwheat
or foxtail)
2 tbsp olive oil or any
local oil
1 large onion
2 large tomatoes
2 green chillies
1 tsp ginger–garlic paste
1 tsp sambhar masala
(p. 193)
A handful of coriander
stems/leaves
1 cucumber
1 bell pepper
2 small red radishes
1 stalk of spring onion

For the dressing
Juice of 2 small lemons
3 tbsp olive oil
1–2 fresh red chillies
1 tbsp mint leaves
2 tbsp coriander leaves
Salt and pepper to taste

For garnish
Lemon wedges, chillies,
amaranth pops and black
rice pops

METHOD

1 Wash the millets a minimum of three times to remove the bitterness.
2 Take the millets and double the amount of water in a pot and cook over medium heat for 15–20 minutes. Take the millets off the heat and spread them out in a big tray. Pour 1 tbsp olive oil and mix.
3 Slice the onions, tomatoes and green chillies. Finely chop the remaining vegetables and keep aside.
4 In a pan, add 1 tbsp oil and fry the ginger–garlic paste and sambhar masala. Once the paste is ready add the millets.
5 For the dressing, combine all the ingredients in a small bowl. If you want to add some chilli sauce or vinegar, add it now.
6 Toss the warm millets and vegetables with the dressing and serve!

Chicken Farcha

preparation time **30 minutes** serves **4–6**

INGREDIENTS

1 kg chicken thighs
(boneless) or chicken leg
pieces, cut in half

For the marination

2 tbsp ginger–garlic
paste
1 tsp red chilli powder
1 tsp turmeric powder
1 tsp sambhar masala
2 tbsp lemon juice
Salt and pepper to taste

For the coating

4 eggs
1 cup fresh breadcrumbs
Salt and pepper to taste
Oil for deep frying

METHOD

1 Wash and dry the chicken.
2 Combine all the ingredients for the marination in a large bowl and marinate the chicken. Refrigerate overnight or at least for a couple of hours.
3 When ready to eat, get your frying station together. Put a deep pot with oil over a medium to high flame. The marinated chicken should be at room temperature. Set aside a plate with a kitchen paper towel to soak excess oil.
4 Beat the eggs in a bowl, season with salt and pepper.
5 In a shallow plate or large bowl, season the breadcrumbs with salt and pepper.
6 Dip the marinated chicken in the beaten eggs, then coat with the breadcrumbs and fry. Let the chicken cook on both sides for 5–10 minutes. To check if the chicken is cooked, pierce it with a knife. The blade should come out easily.
7 Drain the excess oil on a paper towel and serve the chicken hot with lemon, green chutney (p. 89) and some onions.

Fried Fish

preparation time **4 hours** serves **4**

INGREDIENTS

500 g of any fresh fish

For the marination
1 tsp turmeric powder
1 tsp red chilli powder
1 tsp sambhar masala (p.
193) If you don't have it,
add some chilli–garlic
paste (p. 192)
Salt to taste
Juice of 2 lemons
½ cup whole wheat flour
(atta) for coating
¼ cup of oil for shallow
frying

METHOD

1 Wash and pat the fish dry with a paper towel, then cut it
   into pieces (roughly 80 g each).
2 In a bowl, mix the dry spices, salt and lemon juice.
   Marinate the fish in this mixture for 30 minutes to an
   hour.
3 In a shallow frying pan, add a little oil and heat well.
4 Coat a piece of fish in the flour and shallow fry on
   medium to high flame till golden on one side, then turn
   and cook on the other side. It should take 8–10 minutes.
5 Place the fried fish on paper to drain the excess oil. Serve
   hot with green chutney (p. 89) and lemon. If you like,
   sprinkle some chaat masala on top.

TIP If you want to use boneless fish, then rawas (Indian
salmon) and surmai (seer fish) are the best options; if with
bone, then pomfret is great.

Jardaloo Sali Murgi

CHICKEN WITH APRICOTS
preparation time **1 hour** serves **4**

INGREDIENTS

1 kg chicken thigh, with bone
2 tbsp ginger–garlic paste
20-25 dried whole apricots
¼ cup oil
2 onions, finely chopped
4 green chillies, slit
1 tsp sambhar masala (p. 193)
1 tsp garam masala
1 tsp red chilli powder
1 tsp turmeric powder
1 tsp cumin powder
1 tsp coriander powder
5 tomatoes, finely chopped
1 tsp jaggery powder
2 tsp Kolah (or any other) vinegar
Salt to taste

For garnish

Salli (potato sticks) and fresh coriander leaves

METHOD

1 Marinate the chicken with ginger–garlic paste and salt for 30 minutes.
2 Soak the dried apricots in 1 cup water (or until covered) and 1 tsp vinegar, then remove the seeds. (Keep the water to cook the chicken, it will add flavour.)
3 Heat oil in a large pan. Add the onions and fry till brown.
4 Add the green chillies and all the dry masalas, and bhuno well.
5 Add the tomatoes and cook for another 10 minutes, until the masala mix is soft and well cooked.
6 Add the marinated chicken to the masala and mix well.
7 Add ½ cup water (including the water leftover from soaking the apricots) and cook the chicken till almost done.
8 Add the apricots and cook for another 5–10 minutes.
9 Once the chicken is tender, add the jaggery and 1 tsp vinegar; check the salt and add if required. The chicken should be tangy, spicy and sweet to taste.
10 Garnish with chopped coriander and lots of salli and serve.

TIP Chicken thigh with bone is best for this, but you can use boneless chicken too.
Swap the chicken with paneer, marinated and pan seared, for a vegetarian option.

Kid Gosht

MUTTON IN CASHEWNUT AND COCONUT GRAVY
preparation time **2 hours** serves **4–6**

INGREDIENTS

1 kg mutton (pichla raan/
back leg), cut into curry
pieces

2 tbsp ginger–garlic
paste

Salt to taste

100 g cashewnuts

1 cup milk

1 cup thick coconut milk

½ tsp nutmeg powder

½ tsp cinnamon powder

½ tsp black pepper
powder

2 onions, finely sliced

3 whole green chillies, slit

1 medium-size
cinnamon stick

4–5 cloves

4–5 black peppercorns

2 green cardamoms

2 bay leaves

4 large potatoes

4 tbsp oil

Fresh coriander and
birista (p. 194) for garnish

METHOD

1 Marinate the mutton with ginger–garlic paste and salt for 5–6 hours.

2 Soak the cashewnuts in ½ cup of warm water, for half an hour, until soft.

3 Grind the cashewnuts into a paste and mix it with milk. Add the coconut milk (reserve some to drizzle for garnish) and powdered spices to this milk mixture. Set aside.

4 In a pressure cooker, add 2 tsp oil and the mutton and stir and seal the meat. Add 2 cups water and cook for 4–5 whistles and leave it on simmer for 15 minutes.

5 In another kadhai, heat 2 tsp oil and add the whole spices. Once they bloom, add the green chillies and onions and sauté till translucent.

6 Add the cooked mutton to the kadhai and pour the cashewnut mixture. You should get the subtle taste of the spices and strong flavour of black pepper.

7 Peel, quarter and deep-fry the potatoes till crispy. Add them to the mutton, cover and cook for a few more minutes till the gravy thickens.

8 Once cooked, remove and garnish with some birista, chopped coriander and a drizzle of coconut milk. Enjoy with steamed rice or garam rotli.

Salli Boti

preparation time **1 hour** serves **4–6**

INGREDIENTS

1 kg mutton (pichla raan/
back leg, cut into pieces)
2 tbsp ginger–garlic
paste
4 onions, chopped
4 tbsp oil
3 tomatoes, chopped
Salt to taste
2–3 bay leaves
2–3 star anise
1 medium-size
cinnamon stick
1 tsp red chilli powder
1 tsp turmeric powder
1 tsp coriander powder
1 tsp cumin powder
1 tsp dhana-jiru (p. 193)
or garam masala
1 tsp sambhar masala
(p. 193)
1 tbsp jaggery powder
1 tbsp Kolah (or any
other) vinegar
Chopped coriander for
garnish
Salli on top

METHOD

1 In a pressure cooker, heat the oil. Add the whole spices and then the chopped onion. Sauté till golden brown.
2 Add the ginger–garlic paste and all the powdered spices. Mix well.
3 Add the mutton and sear it well.
4 Now, add the tomatoes and 2 cups of water. Close the lid and cook the meat for 4–5 whistles and 15 minutes on simmer.
5 Open the lid and continue to cook till the gravy thickens slightly.
6 Lastly, add the vinegar and jaggery and let it boil for another 5 minutes.
7 Garnish with coriander, top with salli and serve hot with toasted pav.

Parsi Chicken Cutlets

preparation time **1 hour** serves **4**

INGREDIENTS

500 g chicken mince

1 tsp oil

1 tsp cumin seeds

1 tbsp ginger-garlic paste

Salt and pepper to taste

1 cup water

1 onion, chopped

2 tbsp fresh coriander, chopped

2 green chillies, chopped

2 green chillies, chopped

1 tsp each of red chilli powder, coriander powder and jeera powder (optional)

For the coating

2 eggs

Breadcrumbs as required

Oil for shallow frying

METHOD

1   In a pan set over medium heat, add the oil and cumin seeds. Once the seeds begin to splutter, add the chicken mince and fry.

2   Mix well, add ginger-garlic paste and salt and pepper.

3   Mix in 1 cup of water and bring the mince to a boil. Once the mince has cooked completely and all the water has been absorbed, turn off the heat and let it cool to room temperature.

4   Grind the mince in a mixie.

5   In another bowl, break the eggs and beat well.

6   Add half of the egg to the ground-up mince along with the chopped onion, coriander and green chillies. If you are adding the powdered spices, you should do so now.

7   Mix well and shape into 40 g cutlets.

8   Dip the cutlets into the remaining egg, coat with breadcrumbs and fry until nice and golden. Serve hot with tomato or green chutney (p. 89). And if you don't have that, ketchup works just fine!

TIP Swap chicken with soy kheema for a vegetarian option.

Kheema Pav

preparation time **1 hour** serves **4–6**

INGREDIENTS

1 kg mutton/chicken
mince
4 tbsp oil
1 tbsp ginger-garlic paste
2 large onions, chopped
3 large tomatoes,
chopped or 1 cup tomato
puree
Salt to taste
1 tsp red chilli powder
1 tsp turmeric powder
1 tsp coriander powder
1 tsp cumin powder
1 tsp sambhar masala
(p. 193)
2 tbsp Kolah (or any
other) vinegar
2 tbsp jaggery powder
Chopped coriander for
garnish

METHOD

1 Heat the oil in a kadhai/pan, add the onions and fry till
golden brown.
2 Add the ginger-garlic paste, all the dry masalas and fry
well.
3 Add the mince and salt and cook, stirring frequently
until the water from the mince has evaporated. Add
the tomatoes and 1 cup water and cook till it all comes
together (about 20 minutes).
4 In a separate bowl, mix the vinegar and jaggery. Add it
to the mince and let it cook for another 5 minutes. Serve
hot, garnished with coriander leaves.

TIP Best eaten with hot butter toasted pav, some freshly
cut onions, a slice of lemon and topped with salli (potato
sticks).

Narial Doodh Ma Cauliflower

preparation time **45 minutes** serves **4**

INGREDIENTS

1 cauliflower, cut into
      florets
3 tbsp oil (preferably
      coconut)/ghee
Salt to taste
2 onions, sliced
1 medium-size
      cinnamon stick
3-4 cloves
1-2 green cardamom
2 bay leaves
1 tsp ginger–garlic paste
3-4 green chillies, slit
1-2 dried red chilli
      powder
½ tsp nutmeg powder
½ tsp cinnamon powder
½ tsp black pepper
      powder
2 cups coconut milk
Curry leaves for garnish

METHOD

1   In a pan, add the oil/ghee and heat well. Add the whole spices and let them bloom for a minute or two.
2   Add the sliced onion and sauté with a bit of salt.
3   Add the green chillies and ginger–garlic paste and fry for 1 minute.
4   Add the cauliflower and ½ cup water and bring it to a boil.
5   Once the cauliflower is almost cooked, add the coconut milk and cook till the stems are soft.
6   Add the powdered spices. Give it another boil.
7   Once the gravy has thickened slightly, garnish with curry leaves and serve hot with rotli or pav.

Bhaji Dana

preparation time **30 minutes** serves **2**

INGREDIENTS

100 g spinach leaves
100 g methi leaves
1 large onion, chopped
2 green chillies, chopped
1 tsp ginger–garlic paste
1 tsp dhana-jiru masala
(p. 193)
½ tsp red chilli powder
1 tsp cumin seeds
½ tsp grated nutmeg
50 g boiled green peas
Salt to taste
1 tbsp coriander,
chopped

METHOD

1 Wash and clean all the greens. Roughly chop the spinach leaves.
2 In a pan, add oil and the onions and sauté until golden.
3 Add the ginger–garlic paste, green chillies and all the spices. Cook till aromatic.
4 Add the spinach and methi and sauté for 3–4 minutes or until they wilt.
5 Add the peas, season with salt and cook for another 3–4 minutes till the water evaporates.
6 Add the coriander and serve hot with rotli or as a healthy side dish with dal–chawal!

TIP If you find it slightly bitter, add a dash of lemon!

Chutney Pattice

preparation time **45 minutes** serves **4–6**

INGREDIENTS

1 kg potatoes
Salt and pepper to taste
2 tbsp plain flour (maida)
Oil for shallow frying

For the coating

4 tbsp corn flour + 8 tbsp
of water to make a slurry
1 cup fresh breadcrumbs

For the filling

250 g green chutney
(p. 89)

METHOD

1 Prepare the chutney and keep aside.
2 Boil the potatoes with the skin on. Once they're cooked, peel and mash them with flour and salt.
3 With slightly wet hands, take a scoop of mashed potato (the size of a golf ball) and fill 1 tsp chutney in the centre. Form a ball and flatten a bit, like a tikki. (If they don't hold shape and your potato is too wet, then keep it in the fridge till it hardens, it'll make it easier to fry.)
4 Repeat with the rest of the potatoes.
5 Dip the pattice in the cornflour slurry and then coat them with breadcrumbs.
6 Heat oil in a pan and fry the pattice on both sides, till golden brown. Serve hot as a tea-time snack or an appetizer.

Mawa Cake

preparation time **1 hour** serves **8**

INGREDIENTS

1⅓ cup flour (maida)

1 cup butter

2 cups icing sugar

½ cup milk

5 eggs

½ capful vanilla essence

250 g fresh mawa

1 tsp baking powder

METHOD

1 Preheat oven to 180°C.

2 In a mixing bowl, cream the butter and sugar. Then add the eggs one by one.

3 Add the vanilla essence and mix well.

4 In another bowl, combine the flour, icing sugar and baking powder. Sieve and keep aside.

5 Fold the dry ingredients into the wet ingredients slowly.

6 Add the mawa and milk, and mix well.

7 Once the batter is ready, fill into cups and bake for 15–20 minutes. (If you are using a big mould, it will take 45–50 minutes.) Cool and serve.

Dhun's Caramel Custard

preparation time **1 hour** serves **4**

INGREDIENTS

For the caramel
200 g sugar

For the custard
8 whole eggs
4 egg yolks (this is the trick to extra creaminess)
1.1 litre milk
200 g sugar
Vanilla essence as per taste (a vanilla pod will give you a stronger flavour)
Fresh strawberries (or a compote) for garnish

METHOD

1   Pre-heat your oven to 160-180°C. Keep your custard moulds ready. Two 4–inch or one 8–inch mould works fine. If you prefer making one large bowl of custard, steam bake for about 30-40 minutes.

2   To make the caramel, melt the sugar in a pan over medium heat. Don't add any water or milk, just heat the sugar till it is a light golden colour. Pour the caramel into the mould and leave it to harden.

3   To make the custard, combine all the ingredients in a bowl and whisk well. Fine strain the entire mixture to make sure there are no lumps.

4   Pour into the mould and cover with a lid or aluminum foil if needed.

5   Steam bake the custard in a bain marie (water bath) for 25-30 minutes. If you are using smaller moulds, the custard will be ready in 12-15 minutes. Don't overcook it.

6   Cool the caramel custard at room temperature, then chill. Once chilled well, demould and serve with strawberries (or any fruit compote).

TIP You can add a pinch of elaichi-jaiphal, a green cardamom and nutmeg powder, which is a typically Parsi thing to do, instead of vanilla.

Old-school Piped Butter Cookies (Eggless)

preparation time **15 minutes** makes **12 cookies**

INGREDIENTS

80 g flour (maida)

40 g sugar

1½ tsp corn flour (or 40 g icing sugar)

60 g butter

15 ml milk

A pinch of salt

½ tsp vanilla essence

METHOD

1 Pre-heat oven to 175°C.

2 In a bowl, cream the butter and sugar till pale.

3 Add the milk and vanilla and mix well.

4 Sieve all the dry ingredients into a bowl.

5 Mix the wet and dry ingredients together till just combined.

6 Transfer the batter into a piping bag fitted with a star nozzle and pipe. Bake for 12-15 minutes.

7 Once cooled, decorate with your favourite jam.

Mom's Chocolate Cake

preparation time **1 hour** serves **6**

INGREDIENTS

For the cake
1¾ cup flour (maida)
2 cups sugar
¾ cup cocoa powder
1 tsp baking powder
2 tsp baking soda
A pinch of salt
2 eggs
1 cup milk + 1 tbsp white vinegar
½ cup oil
1 cup boiling water + 2 tsp instant coffee powder

For the ganache
1 cup dark chocolate, chopped
(I use Mason & Co)
1 cup heavy cream
A pinch of salt
1 tbsp butter

METHOD

1   Preheat the oven to 180°C. Prepare an 8-inch round mould by lining it with parchment paper.

2   Combine all the dry ingredients in a large mixing bowl.

3   In a small bowl, mix the vinegar with the milk. It will curdle, but don't worry—we want that.

4   In another bowl, mix the coffee powder with the boiling water and keep aside.

5   Now add the milk and coffee mixtures, eggs, oil and vanilla essence to the dry mix. Beat well.

6   Pour the batter into the mould and bake for 45-55 minutes.

7   Meanwhile, melt the chocolate in a double boiler.

8   Add the cream and stir to combine.

9   Add the salt and butter and mix well. Set aside till it thickens slightly.

10 Remove the cake from the oven when it is done. Let it cool, then frost with the ganache (or your favourite icing).

Parsi Pantry

THERE'S NO GREATER JOY THAN A KITCHEN WELL-STOCKED WITH MASALAS, CHEESES, OILS AND OTHER STAPLES. TO WHIP UP A QUICK PARSI MEAL, STOCK UP ON THESE ESSENTIAL INGREDIENTS

PASTES THAT PACK A PUNCH

You can always use store bought, but I prefer making these easy-peasy pastes. Store in a clean, dry glass container and refrigerate for up to a month.

Adu Lasan Nu Paste

This ginger–garlic paste is a 3:2 ratio (60 per cent garlic and 40 per cent ginger). Wash the ingredients and let them dry on the kitchen slab. Roughly chop them and then, using a mixer, grind to a thickish paste. When grinding, add a little bit of oil (no water). When storing, pour oil on top to seal it so it lasts longer.

Chilli-Garlic Paste

Take 10-12 large red chillies (whatever variety you like – I use dried Kashmiri chillies) and soak in warm water for a few hours. Peel two whole garlic pods. Drain the chillies and, in a mixer, grind them with the garlic till you get a smooth paste. Use to spice up any dish.

Lasan-Jeeru Paste

Take two bulbs of garlic, peeled and cleaned, 1 tbsp of roasted whole cumin seeds and 2-3 green chillies in a mixer. Grind with a little water to a smooth paste. When storing, pour oil on top to seal it so it lasts longer.

SPICE BOX

The late Bhicoo J. Manekshaw has been a huge inspiration for me. I was lucky enough to meet her and get my copy of *Parsi Food and Customs* signed. A Le Cordon Bleu graduate, she regaled me with tales, including the one about her Kera Per Eeda recipe earning her that coveted thirteenth spot in class. Her masala recipes which I've shared below are gold!

Garam Masala Powder

15 g whole cinnamon, 10 g cloves, 15 g green cardamom, 10 g black peppercorn, 100 g cumin seeds (optional)

Clean spices, dry roast them and grind to a powder. Store in a clean dry jar.

Dhana-Jiru Masala

1-inch piece turmeric, 50 g curry leaves, 250 g cumin seeds, 60 g caraway seeds, 1 kg coriander seeds, 50 g fenugreek seeds, 50 g cinnamon, 50 g cloves, 50 g green cardamom, 200 g black peppercorn, 50 g poppy seeds, 50 g bay leaves, 50 g dried orange peel (with pith removed), 50 g dried sweet lime peel (with pith removed)

Roast each ingredient individually with 1-2 tsp of oil (for each ingredient) on a tava. Cool, grind and store in an airtight container. This can be kept for a year.

Sambhar Masala

200 g Kashmiri red chillies (or you could use chilli powder), 100 g mustard seeds, 250 g fenugreek seeds, 20 g asafoetida powder, 20 g cinnamon, 20 g cloves, 20 g black peppercorns, 100 g star anise, 1 tsp salt, 2 tbsp oil

Grind all the spices, except asafoetida, individually. Transfer the powders to a large thali and mix thoroughly. Make a well in the centre and place the asafoetida in it. Heat the oil till very hot and pour it over the asafoetida. Crush it completely with a wooden spoon. Mix well and cool. Store in an airtight glass jar.

Curry Powder

75 g dried red chillies (a mixture of Kashmiri, Goa and any local chilli), 50 g turmeric powder, 75 g dry ginger powder, 75 g dry garlic powder, 200 g cumin seeds, 10 g bay leaves, 10 g curry leaves, 400 g small coriander seeds, 75 g mustard seeds, 100 g fenugreek seeds, 100 g poppy seeds, 250 g roasted gram, 100 g star anise, 50 g black sesame seeds, 5 g cinnamon, 5 g cloves, 5 g green cardamom (weighed and peeled), 10 g black peppercorn, 2 nutmegs, 5 g salt, 2 tbsp oil

Wash and dry coriander, cumin and fenugreek seeds individually as they are usually full of dust. Dry roast and grind each ingredient separately, then mix together. Heat the oil till it's very hot, sprinkle onto spice powder and mix well. This preserves the masala for a longer time. Store in an airtight glass container.

IN MY LARDER/FRIDGE

Eggs The backbone of Parsi food (see p. 55).

Ghee The generation before us did a lot of cooking in desi ghee. It's the best kind of flavour and fat.

Vinegar Kolah vinegar, made from sugarcane, is a Parsi mainstay but I'd also recommend stocking up on apple cider, white and coconut vinegar.

Flavouring Pure rose water, vanilla essence and saffron are used to enhance the flavour of our food.

Fried Nuts I always have a jar of fried almonds, cashewnuts, raisins and chironji in my fridge to use as a garnish for pulao, Ravo, etc.

Fresh Malai I skim it off the top of whole cream milk and store.

Tamarind Paste A souring agent used in patio, Prawn Curry and Vindaloo.

Dried Methi Leaves I usually buy fresh fenugreek (methi) leaves when in season. After they've been washed and sun-dried on a newspaper, I crush and store them in a jar to use in Dhansak.

Birista Here's the recipe – take 7-8 medium-sized onions and oil for deep frying. The secret to crispy fried onions is thin slicing. Heat oil in a kadhai, and add the onions in small batches. The oil should be hot enough to make the onions sizzle. Fry without stirring too much till they are a light brown colour. Switch off the heat and let the onions continue to brown in the oil. Remove the onions and drain in a large sieve. Then spread them on a flat surface and allow them to cool and crisp up. Store in an airtight container.

SAY CHEERS!

I usually have white wine at home; it goes really well with spicy Parsi food. Fratelli Sette, a red wine, pairs beautifully with heavy Indian food.

Kingfisher beer with afternoon lunch.

Parsi women love their cocktails—vodka-tonic with slice of chilli or fruit is a hot fave.

Meal Plan Ideas

BREAKFAST

Ravo (p. 27) + Akuri (p. 66) + hot buttered
toast + Parsi Choi (p. 51)

Leela Lasan Nu Eedu (p. 65) + leftover
rotli + Pheteli coffee (p. 53) + fruits

LUNCH

Parsi Chicken Cutlets (p. 179) + Dhansak
(p. 131) + Caramel Custard (p. 187)

Chutney Pattice (p. 184) + Kairi Chicken
(p. 39) + rotli + Falooda (p. 171)

Dhan Dar (p. 99) + Prawn or Vengna Nu
patio (p. 99) + Fried Boomla (p. 155) +
Ravo (p. 27)

Prawn Curry Rice (p. 115) + Chutney
Pattice (p. 184) + Falooda (p. 171)

Salli Kheema (p. 181) + Dhan Dar (p. 99) +
Caramel Custard (p. 187)

Dhan Dar (p. 99) + Fried Fish (p. 175) +
Ravo (p. 27)

TEA-TIME

Butter Cookies (p. 188) + Mawa Cake (p.
185) + Parsi Choi + Pheteli Coffee (p. 51) +
Mom's Chocolate Cake (p. 189)

DINNER

Kid Gosht (p. 177) / Narial Doodh Ma
Cauliflower (p. 182) + rotli + Bhaji Dana (p.
183) + Ravo (p. 27)

Pork Vindaloo (p. 77) + Fresh Pav (p. 141) +
Khara Bheeda (p. 165) + Mawa Cake (p. 185)

Patra Ni Machchi (p. 89) + rotli + Rainbow
Millet Salad (p. 172)

Berry Pulav (Chicken/Mutton/Veg) (p. 143)
+ Chicken Farcha (p. 173) + Falooda (p. 171)

Salli Boti (p. 178) + Fresh Pav (p. 141) +
Khara Bheeda (p. 165) + Ravo (p. 27)

Jardalu Chicken (p. 176) + Fried Fish (p.
175) + Dhun's Caramel Custard (p. 187) +
Fresh Pav (p. 141)

Glossary

Aam mango
Achaar pickle
Adrakh-lasan ginger–garlic
Alu Gobi potato-cauliflower preparation
Arhar/tuvar, lal masoor, kali masoor dal lentils
Atta wholewheat flour
Badam almonds
Besan chickpea flour
Bhindi, bheeda ladyfinger, okra
Bhonu feast
Bhuna sauté
Birista deep fried onion,
Boomla Bombay duck
Chakhna a savoury dry snack
Chakr phool star anise
Chamna silver pomfret
Chana dal split chickpea
Chironji a nutty seed
Chusiya aam mango varieties like Chausas, Dussehri and Langda that can be slurped
Dalchini cinnamon
Dal-Chawal lentils and rice
Dal ghotni mashing stick
Dhania coriander seeds
Doodh milk
Elaichi cardamom, green or black
Falooda a cold, layered dessert
Ghee clarified butter
Gulkand sweet preserve of rose petals

Gur jaggery
Haldi turmeric
Halwa a rich, sweet preparation
Hara dhaniya Fresh coriander
Hari mirch green chilli
Imli tamarind
Jaiphal nutmeg
Jardaloo apricots
Jeera cumin seeds
Kachumbar simple chopped salad
Kaddu green, red or yellow pumpkin
Kaju cashewnut
Kaju draksh cashew and raisin
Kairi or kachha aam raw mango
Kali mirch black pepper
Kangni foxtail
Kathal jackfruit
Khari biscuit puff pastry biscuit
Kheer rice pudding
Kheema chicken, goat or lamb mince
Khichdi one-pot Indian dish of lentils, rice and spices
Khus-khus poppy seeds
Kesar saffron
Kishmish raisins
Kokam dried fruit with a sharp tangy taste
Kopra coconut
Kuttu buckwheat

Lal mirch red chilli powder
Lauki bottle gourd
Laung cloves
Maida refined flour
Mawa, khoya milk that has been boiled and reduced to a doughy thickness
Methi dana fenugreek seeds
Moong dal bhajia crispy dumpling made with ground lentils, spices and herbs
Mungphali peanuts
Paneer cottage cheese
Pattice crispy patties
Pav bread
Prasad blessed food
Pudina mint
Pulao a rice preparation
Pyaaz-tamatar onion-tomato
Rajgira amaranth
Rawas Indian salmon
Rotla rotli, thin chappati
Sabzi a vegetable preparation
Salli potato sticks
Silbatta grinding stone
Sirka vinegar
Singhara catfish
Suji semolina, rava
Tava flat griddle
Tej patta bay leaf
Til white sesame seeds
Varagu kodo millets

Acknowledgements

Arush Bhandari, my husband and long-time love, who's not only supported me in this journey but pushed me to do more. He's helped me write this book, and without him this would have been incomplete.

My mother, Nilufer N. Dhondy, who not only taught me how to lift a spoon and fork, but also wield a knife in the kitchen. Thank you for being the best head chef anyone could train under and for helping me cook, create and plate most of the recipes here in this book.

My father, Navroze Dhondy, who sometimes gets overshadowed by the strong women in the family because he doesn't cook much. My love of photography and creative writing are a gift from him. Most of the family photographs used here are from his collection over the years.

Both my grandmoms, Meher Dhondy and Vera Ghandhi—every meeting with them as a child, I learnt something, ate something (that goes without saying) and had so much fun.

My talented brother, Kurush Dhondy, who helps me shoot so much of my cooking, and most importantly enjoys eating it!

My in-laws, Anjul and Ashish Bhandari, for their love and constant support. I couldn't have done it without you, Arshita, Sarthak, Bhavya, Kriti and the entire Khurana and Bhandari families.

My friends—Nitya, Saanya, Kanupriya, Shriya—who've always cheered me on and enjoyed my food. Villie Aunty, Jaloo Aunty, and everyone who helped with stories and the recipes for the book.

My teachers at IHM-Aurangabad, Le Cordon Bleu (London), Taj hotels and all my internships, thank you for such enriching experiences and for sharing with me your knowledge of food.

The late Bhicoo J. Manekshaw who showed me the path to taking Parsi food to the globe, thank you for being a true mentor.

A big thank you to Dr Shernaz Cama, Kritika and Vanshika at the Parzor Foundation. Dr Cama, the support you have given me for my research into Parsi culture has been invaluable. To all the people we emailed, and those who got back and helped—Nilufer Mavalwala, Mr Dinshaw Tamboly, Eric and Sarosh Dastoorji, the Sidhwas at Globe Hotel, Freny Aunty in Ahmedabad who helped and guided me on a few classic Parsi recipes—thank you.

Mr AD Singh, Chef Saby, Mohit Balachandaran, Chef Irfan and my entire team at SodaBottleOpenerWala—Pratap, Jaybeer, Birender, Danesh— who have supported me through the years.

Sanjoo Malhotra and Sourish Bhattacharya for introducing me to Paul Newnham and the entire Chefs' Manifesto team which took me around the globe to cook and allowed me to share my love for Parsi food, sustainable gastronomy and represent India on the world stage.

Ananth Padmanabhan, who really believed in me and this book when we had no idea where we were going with it. Thank you for backing my literary dreams.

Diya Kar, who has been there from the start, and Shreya Punj; Bonita Vaz-Shimray and Divya Saxena for your wonderful design. And my editor, Sonal Nerurkar, who has been so patient with me and this book. It's taken me a while to put it together and I'm so happy to see it come to life.

Shiva Kant Vyas and Saumya Gupta, who have worked with me for so many years and understand my aesthetic sense, thank you for your photography and styling skills.

Last, but not the least, all my followers on Instagram who've been with me on my culinary journey, learning, sharing and cooking recipes all through these years. Thank you for sticking around. I've got lots of stuff planned for you.

CREDITS

COVER DESIGN AND BOOK LAYOUT Divya Saxena
COVER PHOTOGRAPHY Nitin Sadana
COVER STYLING Parsi Gara sari by Ashdeen
SUPPORTING PHOTOGRAPHY FOR THE COVER Kurush Dhondy and Dhruv Prakash
PHOTOGRAPHY Saumya Gupta
STYLING Shiva Kant Vyas
SUPPORTING PHOTOGRAPHY Anahita Dhondy/Navroze Dhondy/SodaBottleOpenerWala archives
CROCKERY Courtesy Nilufer N. Dhondy
LOCATION The Dhondy family home
PROJECT EDITOR Sonal Nerurkar
COPY EDITOR Shatarupa Ghoshal
PREPRESS Sanjeev Kumar
ART DIRECTION Bonita Vaz Shimray

About the Author

ANAHITA DHONDY can't remember a time when she wasn't planning on becoming a chef. She pursued her culinary dream first by enrolling into the Institute of Hotel Management, Aurangabad, where she graduated at the top of her class in Culinary Arts. After training at the Taj Group of Hotels and J.W. Marriott, she went on to acquire a Grande Diplome from Le Cordon Bleu, London. On her return to India, at the age of twenty-three, Anahita joined SodaBottleOpenerWala, part of the Olive Group of Restaurants, as Chef Manager.

A champion of Parsi food and of promoting lost recipes and ingredients in her cooking, Anahita has represented India and SodaBottleOpenerWala at the EAT Forum 2018 and the UN-affiliated Chefs' Manifesto in Stockholm and London in 2018. She has won several awards, including the Times Food Guide & Nightlife Award for Noteworthy Newcomer (2013) and Condé Nast Traveller's Innovator of the Year (2018).

In 2019, Anahita featured on *Forbes Asia's* '30 Under 30' list for her contribution towards food sustainability and for popularizing Parsi cuisine.

Anahita enjoys discovering local ingredients, shops and eateries and sharing her amazing finds on her Instagram page (@anahitadhondy) just as much as she enjoys cooking. A Punju-Bawi who cooks Parsi food from the heart, she dreams of popularizing the cuisine she has grown up with while representing India on the world stage.

When she isn't creating recipes and flavours in her head, she likes to read romantic novels, play with her puppy, Yuzu, and dance at every opportunity she gets.